HipHopEd: The Compilation on Hip-Hop Education

Hip-Hop Education

Innovation, Inspiration, Elevation

Edmund Adjapong and Christopher Emdin
General Editors

Vol. 3

The Hip-Hop Education series is part of the Peter Lang Education list.
Every volume is peer reviewed and meets
the highest quality standards for content and production.

PETER LANG
New York • Bern • Berlin
Brussels • Vienna • Oxford • Warsaw

HipHopEd: The Compilation on Hip-Hop Education

Volume 3: Hip-Hop as Resistance and Social and Emotional Learning

Edited by
Ian Levy and Edmund Adjapong

PETER LANG

New York • Bern • Berlin
Brussels • Vienna • Oxford • Warsaw

Library of Congress Control Number: 2018012781

Bibliographic information published by **Die Deutsche Nationalbibliothek.**
Die Deutsche Nationalbibliothek lists this publication in the "Deutsche
Nationalbibliografie"; detailed bibliographic data are available
on the Internet at http://dnb.d-nb.de/.

ISSN 2643-5551 (print)
ISSN 2643-556X (online)
ISBN 978-1-4331-8161-0 (paperback)
ISBN 978-1-4331-8341-6 (ebook pdf)
ISBN 978-1-4331-8342-3 (epub)
DOI 10.3726/b17487

© 2021 Peter Lang Publishing, Inc., New York
80 Broad Street, 5th floor, New York, NY 10004
www.peterlang.com

To our beloved father, Osei Adjapong.
—Edmund

To my incredible parents, Howard and Claudia, and my wonderful wife Joanna.
Thank you for your unwavering love and support.
—Ian

Table of Contents

Introduction

Hip-hop as Resistance and Social and Emotional Learning

IAN LEVY AND EDMUND ADJAPONG

@IanPLevy and @KingAdjapong

For the third volume of The Compilation on Hip-Hop Education, we continue to highlight the voices, stories, and narratives of educators and scholars who approach their practice and research using a framework anchored in hip-hop culture. Much like prior iterations of this series, this edited volume includes chapters from senior scholars, emerging scholars, and practicing educators. As co-editors, our goal is to continue to support and share scholarship that is rooted in hip-hop culture that provides new practical and strategic insights for scholars, practitioners, students, community members, and policymakers as it relates to processing a bevy of life's stressors.

This volume of The Compilation on Hip-Hop Education series highlights the use of *hip-hop as resistance and social and emotional learning* across educational spaces. The chapters in this text are informed by hip-hop theory, practices, and the authors' lived experiences in order to offer individuals approaches as in the development of social and emotional resources to navigate the world at large. Historically, hip-hop positioned itself as a beacon of hope within environments disproportionately fraught with educational and mental health disparities (Emdin et al., 2016; Levy et al., 2018). At its core, hip-hop culture emerged as a counter-narrative and platform for participants to speak back against systemic inequities (Chang, 2005). Scholars have expressed that the beauty of hip-hop is that it "embraces those who have also been excluded from the norm" (Emdin, 2010, p. 6).

However, as hip-hop has grown in prominence and popularity, it is in a constant fight to circumvent cooption and to protect its roots (Rose, 2008). Commercialized hip-hop music, videos, and dances have fed negative stereotypes about the Black and Brown community (Reyna et al., 2009; Yousman, 2003). Scholars have critiqued mainstream media for deliberately portraying a stereotypical perception of hip-hop culture, and thereby supporting the public in adopting an understanding of hip-hop that is removed from its cultural origins (Graham, 2017). In fact, there is substantial fear that this portrayal threatens the erasure of hip-hop's cultural complexities (Thompson, 2016). Given the framing of hip-hop culture as youth culture (Adjapong & Emdin, 2015), we can also be fearful of the erasure of youth's inherent complexities.

Resisting the impact of society on one's personal identity development is at the core of what it means to engage in and with hip-hop culture (Wang, 2012). Hip-hop culture promotes authenticity as resistance by providing its participants with the skills to create new platforms for individuals to showcase their complexities and work through difficult thoughts and feelings (McLeod, 1999; Travis et al., 2019). For example, when schools deploy approaches to pedagogy and counseling that are devoid of youth culture, students who appear to be disengaged in traditional classrooms can be found engaging in lunchroom cyphers where they present emotionally laden rhymes that simultaneously allow them to showcase their brilliance and heal (Emdin et al., 2016; Levy et al., 2018). While a particular school system might label this type of practice as unintellectual or disruptive (Alim, 2011), an individual who can see the complexities of hip-hop culture understands that youth are creating opportunities to learn and heal while resisting educational and pedagogical systems that feel inauthentic.

The erasure of a group's history and cultural origins through the use of colonial practices has been explored extensively by scholars. Smith (2012) describes how educational practices deployed by Western Europeans threatened the very existence of indigenous people's values, beliefs, voice, and knowledge. Through the promotion of an ideology that indigenous youth lacked intellect, education became the vehicle through which "imperialism and colonialism brought complete disorder to colonized peoples, disconnecting them from their histories, their landscapes, their languages, their social relations and their own ways of thinking, feelings and interacting with the world" (p. 29). Within contemporary educational systems, Emdin (2016) argues the these same practices are done onto Black and Brown youth today, and presents the term *neoindigenous* to allow individuals to "understand the oppression these youth experience, the spaces they inhabit, and the ways these phenomena affect what happens in social settings like traditional classrooms" (p. 9).

As a solution, or mechanism, to protect the cultural complexities of hip-hop from erasure, Smith (2012) and Emdin (2016) agree that youth need to be able to tell their own stories, in their own ways, for their own purposes. Within educational spaces, Maxine Greene (2007) further explained that "there has always been a tension between those who depend upon some invisible authority for answers and sanctions and those who have learned to exist in uncertainty, with notions of unrealized possibility rather than the comforts of assurance and predictability" (p. 1). Hip-hop culture is presented as an ideal mechanism to resist cooption, and support the exploration of thoughts and feelings, because it has always stood in direct opposition to *invisible authorities* and created lanes for a community to collectively navigate uncertainties and discover possibilities. #HipHopEd approaches, therefore, offer educators and students pathways to utilize hip-hop culture to address a variety of barriers that attempt to inhibit social/emotional, academic, and career development. In this text, the authors explore how educators and scholars alike can leverage hip-hop to both disrupt education and asocial norms and support students in social and emotional learning. These two distinct sections offer a robust pathway to both advocate for hip-hop culture to exist authentically within schools, and then to use hip-hop culture to address a bevy of social and emotional outcomes.

REFERENCES

Adjapong, E. S., & Emdin, C. (2015). Rethinking pedagogy in urban spaces: Implementing hip-hop pedagogy in the urban science classroom. *Journal of Urban Learning, Teaching, and Research, 11,* 66–77.

Adjapong, E. S., & Levy, I. (Eds.). (2020). *HipHopEd: The Compilation on Hip-hop Education: Volume 2: Hip-hop as Praxis and Social Justice.* New York, NY: Peter Lang Publishing.

Alim, H. S. (2011). Global ill-literacies: Hip hop cultures, youth identities, and the politics of literacy. *Review of Research in Education, 35*(1), 120–146.

Chang, J. (2005). *Can't stop won't stop: A history of the hip-hop generation.* New York, NY: St. Martin's Press.

Emdin, C. (2010). Affiliation and alienation: Hip-hop, rap, and urban science education. *Journal of Curriculum Studies, 42,* 1–25. doi:10.1080/00220270903161118

Emdin, C. (2016). *For White folks who teach in the hood…and the rest of y'all too: Reality pedagogy and urban education.* Boston, MA: Beacon Press.

Emdin, C., & Adjapong, E. S. (Eds.). (2018). *#HipHopEd: The Compilation on Hip-hop Education: Volume 1: Hip-hop as Education, Philosophy, and Practice.* New York, NY: BRILL.

Emdin, C., Adjapong, E., & Levy, I. (2016). Hip-hop based interventions as pedagogy/therapy in STEM: A model from urban science education. *Journal for Multicultural Education, 10*(3), 307–321.

Graham, N. J. (2017). Southern rap and the rhetoric of region. *Phylon, 54*(2), 41–57. https://www.jstor.org/stable/10.2307/90018661

Greene, M. (2007). *Toward a Pedagogy of Thought and a Pedagogy of Imagination.* https://maxinegreene.org/uploads/library/toward_pt.pdf.

Levy, I., Emdin, C., & Adjapong, E. (2018). Hip-hop cypher in group work. *Social Work with Groups, 41*(1–2), 103–110. doi: 10.1080/01609513.2016.1275265

McLeod, K. (1999). Authenticity within hip-hop and other cultures threatened with assimilation. *Journal of Communication, 49*, 134–150. doi:10.1111/j.1460-2466.1999.tb02821.x

Reyna, C., Brandt, M., & Tendayi Viki, G. (2009). Blame it on hip hop: Anti-rap attitudes as a proxy for prejudice. *Group Processes and Intergroup Relations, 12*(3), 361–380. https://doi.org/https://doi-org.ezproxy.lib.umb.edu/10.1177/1368430209102848

Rose, T. (2008). *The hip hop wars: What we talk about when we talk about hip hop—and why it matters.* Philadelphia, PA: Basic Civitas Books.

Smith, L. T. (2012). *Decolonizing methodologies: Research and indigenous peoples.* London, England: Zed Books.

Travis, R., Gann, E., Crooke, A. H., & Jenkins, S. M. (2019). Hip Hop, empowerment, and therapeutic beat-making: Potential solutions for summer learning loss, depression, and anxiety in youth. *Journal of Human Behavior in the Social Environment, 29*(6), 744–765.

Wang, X. (2012). "I am not a qualified dialect rapper": Constructing hip-hop authenticity in China. *Sociolinguistic Studies, 6*, 333–372. doi:10.1558/sols.v6i2.333

Yousman, B. (2003). Blackophilia and blackophobia: White youth, the consumption of rap music, and white supremacy. *Communication Theory, 13*(4), 366–391. https://doi.org/https://doi-org.ezproxy.lib.umb.edu/10.1111/j.1468-2885.2003.tb00297.x

PART I

Disrupting Education and Social Norms through Hip-Hop

CHAPTER ONE

From Block Parties to Disrupting Social Norms

EDMUND ADJAPONG

@KingAdjapong

Since its inception hip-hop has been known to disrupt social norms. Hip-hop quickly grew from neighborhood breakdancers battling one another at block parties in the South Bronx into a genre of music and art form that provides a glimpse into the experiences and realities of groups of people who have been pushed to the margins of society. In the 1970s, the South Bronx experienced economic despair. Unemployment and poverty were high and so was crime. Urban youth in the South Bronx experienced daily challenges of living in poverty and in communities that were neglected by the rest of society. As a result, urban youth from the South Bronx haphazardly laid the groundwork for a genre of music and culture that now generates billions of dollars globally. Through hip-hop, young people had an opportunity to assert their identities and gain a voice on the national stage. "The Message" by Grandmaster Flash and the Furious Five was the first prominent hip-hop song that garnered mainstream attention. In the song and its accompanying music video, Grandmaster Flash and the Furious Five paint vivid pictures of the stress of inner-city poverty. "The Message" includes narratives of how urban social systems including education, inner-city housing, and health care did not favor inner-city families. It pushed against the social norms of the marginalization of people of color. From Grandmaster Flash and the Furious Five's prominent song "The Message" (1982) to Childish Gambino's song This is America (2018), hip-hop through its music, art and ultimately culture has always disrupted social norms that contribute to the continued marginalization of people of color and imagined a more socially just society.

In this section, authors brilliantly describe how in many ways hip-hop disrupts social norms. Andrea Hunt begins the section with thoughtful consideration for Hip-Hop Intellectualism while challenging higher education's legitimation of knowledge. Andrew Torres provides a narrative of his life and educational journey and demonstrates how he used hip-hop to disrupt social norms through his work as a scholar-practitioner. Napoleon Wells shares an insightful analysis of hip-hop through a framework for identity development and Mariel Buque shares her work of working with historically marginalized communities to make sense of racial trauma. Mariel Buque anchors her scholarship in the work of Lauryn Hill as a way to pay homage to her community of Newark, NJ and the community of the young people that she works with. The authors of the forthcoming section all make a connection between identity and hip-hop and express either how hip-hop was used or can be used to support historically marginalized groups and therefore push back against unjust social norms.

REFERENCES

Edward, F.G. Grandmaster, F., Melle, M., Williams, S., Robinson, J., McLees, D., Clayton, R. (1982). *The message. On the message* [Audio file]. Retrieved from https://open.spotify.com/track/5DuTNKFEjJIySAyJH1yNDU?si=0X18gtn7QdW_SkgJfnNS2g

Glover, D. (2018). *This is America. On this is America* [Audio file]. Retrieved from https://open.spotify.com/track/0b9oOr2ZgvyQu88wzixux9?si=fZ9BKLcRT5SfPOpfySKvDg

CHAPTER TWO

Hip-Hop Intellectualism and the Legitimation of Knowledge in Higher Education

ANDREA N. HUNT

Since its inception, hip-hop has grown into the most consumed genre of music in the United States. This mass success can be seen in history-making accolades such as Kendrick Lamar winning a Pulitzer Prize in music for his album, *Damn*. The growing acceptance of hip-hop is also evidenced in a rich body of research that documents the effectiveness of hip-hop based education with youth in K–12 educational settings and in community-based programming (Irby & Hall, 2011; Love, 2015; Petchauer, 2015). Hip-hop based education at the post-secondary levels often centers on using lyrics as alternative texts (Gosa & Fields, 2012) and performing content analyses and cultural critiques of the dominant themes and imagery in rap music and videos (Petchauer, 2010). Yet, it extends beyond this and can be used as a lens through which students examine racialized and gendered social structures, sexuality, identity, faith, capitalism, misogyny, cultural appropriation, urban policy, and globalization. Other scholars have also demonstrated how hip-hop based education facilitates cross-racial interactions (Sulè, 2015), increases cultural appreciation (Wessel & Wallaert, 2011), and expands students' worldviews (Petchauer, 2011).

How do you actually achieve the gains in achievement and social capital that scholars such as Sulè (2015), Wessel and Wallaert (2011), Petchauer (2011) and others describe in postsecondary settings? One way is through critical hip-hop pedagogy (Akom, 2009), which is a community teaching and collaboration model that brings together faculty and community members as co-facilitators in the learning process. I will use the Sociology of Hip-Hop Culture class at the

University of North Alabama as an example to illustrate this model while addressing the importance of hip-hop intellectualism (Jenkins, 2011) and the legitimation of knowledge (i.e., who is seen as possessing legitimate knowledge in the hip-hop community and in the college classroom). Further, I will explore our own positionality as educators and the importance of building social and cultural capital in both the hip-hop community and in the classroom.

CRITICAL HIP-HOP PEDAGOGY

Before we can fully immerse ourselves in a discussion of critical hip-hop pedagogy, we must begin with Kerber's (2013) conception of the scholarship of teaching. Kerber (2013) argues that the scholarship of teaching is a transformative social practice that is equally concerned with the value and emancipatory potential of what we do as educators. Central to this process is authenticity. However, academia is often structured in a way that encourages fragmented lives where we are alienated from our labor and are no longer connected to our role as educators (Astin & Astin, 2006; Palmer, 1998). Likewise, students navigate between personal and academic communities trying to reconcile who they are as someone inhabiting these different spaces, which can also lead to fragmented and inauthentic lives.

Authenticity through teaching then means that there is a particular way that we engage with our craft that leads to our own authenticity and, because of this, a way that we engage students that leads to their authenticity. Kerber (2013) asserts that authenticity leads to social justice in higher education that will eventually result in social justice through higher education. We cannot expect students to go out into the world and make a change if they are a part of institutions that do not care about them or their 'being' – we have to help students grow in their own authenticity. This is the promise of hip-hop and where critical hip-hop pedagogy fits into the conversation.

Hip-hop based education is influenced by critical and culturally relevant pedagogy (Irby & Hall, 2011; Ladson-Billings, 1995, 2014) that uses hip-hop to validate knowledge of self and community (Love, 2018; Prier & Beachum, 2008). Because of this, there is a certain level of social responsibility when using hip-hop in educational settings. This social responsibility stems from the historical and contemporary patterns of hip-hop as the primary site for marginalized youth to negotiate their identities. Hip-hop has also served as a space for youth to analyze the dominant social institutions and oppressive practices that affect their lives (Gosa & Fields, 2012; Prier & Beachum, 2008).

Critical hip-hop pedagogy as conceptualized by Akom (2009) and elaborated on by Love (2018) is transdisciplinary and addresses social inequalities, experiential knowledge, and social justice. Critical hip-hop pedagogy draws heavily on Freire's

(1968/1970) critique of the educational system and his pedagogy of the oppressed that encourages youth to engage in a critical praxis of reflection and action to counter the dominant models of schooling that are designed to reproduce inequality. Critical hip-hop pedagogy is also connected to cultural sustaining pedagogies (Paris & Alim, 2014) and based upon asset pedagogies where language, literacies, and ways of being in marginalized communities are seen as assets rather than deficits. Among this family of pedagogies, the goal is to sustain the notion of different ways of learning by creating linguistic, literate, and cultural pluralism. Another central component of these pedagogies is the need for critical reflexivity to see how as educators we are achieving linguistic, literate, and cultural pluralism and to examine our own biases and ways of being that shape our classrooms. These pedagogies have been vital in reframing the experiences of students of color and moving conversations of equity and access from the margins to the center of educational practices. While the focus is on marginalized students and not concerned with the White gaze (i.e., seeing and experiencing the world through the White viewpoint or lens), Paris and Alim (2014) argue these practices should not be hidden beyond the White gaze. These pedagogies can be used with all students as a way to analyze oppressive practices, cultural and linguistic diversity, and achieve higher consciousness which is needed for all students in an increasingly multicultural and globalized society.

Akom (2009) posits a model of learning through critical hip-hop pedagogy that is participatory, committed to co-learning and co-facilitating, involves local capacity building, and empowers all participants. This means that educators and students are empowered through teaching to be their authentic selves (Kerber, 2013) and are connected to teaching and learning as emancipatory and transformative processes. Using elements of critical hip-hop pedagogy, the next section reflects on teaching a Sociology of Hip-Hop Culture class at a regional institution in the South. The goal is to illustrate how you can create physical and intellectual space within higher education to examine systems of oppression and develop critical problem-solving skills that address some of the most pressing social problems today.

REFLECTIONS ON THE SOCIOLOGY OF HIP-HOP CULTURE

The University of North Alabama (UNA) is a predominantly White state regional institution located on the banks of the Tennessee River. Traditional folklore of the Yuchie Tribe, who made their home in the Tennessee River valley, described the waterway as the "the singing river" because of the flowing waters that sounded like a woman singing. It is the birthplace of W.C. Handy and known for the Muscle Shoals sound. Greats such as Aretha Franklin, Etta James, Clarence Carter,

Wilson Pickett, Ottis Redding, and Percy Sledge all traveled to the Shoals area and were inspired by the singing river to record numerous hits at FAME Studios. The music history in this area is well documented, but hip-hop has been left out of this narrative until more recently. On August 28, 2018, the Alabama Music Hall of Fame unveiled its first hip-hop exhibit curated by Slow Motion Soundz Co-Founder Codie G and featuring Geoffrey "G-Mane" Robinson who are both regular guests to the hip-hop culture class at UNA.

The Sociology of Hip-Hop Culture class at UNA is influenced by Lisa Munson's work at Florida State University and others who have been instrumental in bridging hip-hop with the teaching of sociology and other disciplines at the postsecondary level. The course focuses on the formation, growth, and current state of hip-hop culture through a sociological lens. Students learn how to think critically and sociologically about hip-hop culture and its place in society and develop a clearer understanding of the history and social significance of hip-hop culture. In doing so, students are able to describe the cultural significance of hip-hop music in the United States and globally, identify the social, economic, and political aspects of hip-hop and rap music and how these dynamics affect our society and analyze the relationship between hip-hop culture and social change. Since my background is in advocacy and juvenile justice programming, there is a specific focus on how hip-hop has and still does give marginalized youth a platform to share their lived experiences.

For a class like this to be successful, you must first ground it within historical, local, and global contexts. While my class draws heavily on the early development of hip-hop and the social and political climate at the time, it is vital for students to see that hip-hop culture spans geographic spaces and developed within many communities across the nation and globally. Not all of these early artists achieved mainstream commercial success and students today may not be aware of them. However, they were instrumental in shaping the local and regional narratives around hip-hop and their legacy can be seen in the communities of practice that they helped create for artists today. Framing a course in this manner helps shift the conversation away from equating hip-hop culture with contemporary rap music and to a more nuanced consideration of hip-hop intellectualism and the legitimation of knowledge.

Hip-Hop Intellectualism

Within educational settings, hip-hop is often framed as absent of intellectualism and because of this, it is devalued and not considered a legitimate form of knowledge (Akom, 2009; Rodríguez, 2009). This stems from the critiques of hip-hop as supporting violence, hypermasculinity, homophobia, and misogyny (Hill, 2009; Rose, 2008). While critiques of lyrics are prevalent, the lyrics are also a window into the lived realities of poverty and oppression within marginalized communities. Unfortunately, stereotypical imagery commercialized through popular culture is the dominant narrative because it sells more records and streaming subscriptions than critical consciousness and Black intellectualism, especially among White audiences.

Rodríguez (2009) argues that marginalized youth are few opportunities for active dialogue in educational settings so hip-hop culture emerged as a site of inquiry that helped facilitate a dialogue with the world. As such, hip-hop serves as an alternative space for African American intellectualism and knowledge production outside of the academy (Petchauer, 2015; Prier & Beachum, 2008). Using critical hip-hop pedagogy as a foundation for the course, my job as an educator is to create a space for hip-hop intellectualism in the academy and to unpack issues of social inequality. Jenkins (2011) argues that hip-hop is a writing-intensive field where "written and verbal communication are the two primary forms of work production" so the mind or intellect of the artist should be valued. Jenkins' (2011) assertion is based on the premise that artists as writers use poetic elements, literary devices, complex rhyme schemes, and depth in their lyrics to tell a story. This is not to say that all artists write in this manner or care to – some artists just rap while others embody hip-hop culture.

Critical hip-hop pedagogy's focus on co-learning, co-facilitating, and local capacity building (Akom, 2009) directly shape my approach to teaching. This is why I am not the "sage on the stage" in the classroom but the "guide on the side" and share classroom space with local and regional artists. This involves constructing a syllabus and course schedule with co-facilitation and co-collaboration in mind. When working with local hip-hop artists, I share the syllabus with them and identify topics that may coincide with their area of expertise. We create mutual goals for the class period and we discuss the academic readings that were assigned to students. The artist is given autonomy over that class period and can create materials or activities, with my assistance, to engage students in discussion. This past semester we had seven different guest speakers and other additional guests were in the audience on these days. Five out of the seven guest speakers were local artists and they covered topics such as activism, youth programming, intellectualism, religion, and regional identities. The importance of sharing space in the classroom with local artists is that it contributes to the legitimation of knowledge in the academy and creates a sense of authenticity in what we are doing.

This class has become more than a class; it has turned into a movement in the local area. From this class, I collaborated with a faculty member in the art department and local community organizers to host the Quad Cities Urban Arts Expo, which highlighted graffiti and street art in our area. I organized writing workshops for youth that are co-facilitated with Lee Murkey, a local hip-hop artist, and we will begin collecting data together on a new research project examining how hip-hop artists see their role in constructing dominant messages around gender and sexuality. All of this work is grounded within critical hip-hop pedagogy and is part of a community teaching and collaboration model that disrupts systems of oppression, including higher education, and dissenters White experiences and White voices (Gosa & Fields, 2012).

Positionality and Building Social and Cultural Capital

How did I, as a White cisgender woman, come to teach the Sociology of Hip-Hop Culture? I am not an artist, and I make that clear to my students. I am a public sociologist and my areas of training in sociology center on inequality, which is the lens through which I teach. I spent several years as a research assistant on an Office of Juvenile Justice and Delinquency Prevention grant evaluating juvenile aftercare programs in Mobile and Baldwin counties in South Alabama. As a White woman and an avid hip-hop fan, I used my knowledge of hip-hop to develop rapport and trust with the youth I was collecting data from, who were mostly African American. This experience gave me additional cultural capital and laid the foundation for the community work that I continue to do today which involves using hip-hop with youth as a way for them to examine their own lived experiences (Elligan, 2000; Kobin & Tyson, 2006). My previous research examined how hip-hop shapes the identity development of college students with a particular focus on the social construction of gender, race, and sexuality. My current research with Lee Murkey shifts the focus to the artist perspective. I tell you all of this to show that I found my way to this class through a combination of my love for hip-hop, my deep passion for working with youth, and my research and teaching in the area of inequality.

Do my experiences allow me to draw on insider knowledge (Bourke, 2014)? Am I really an insider to hip-hop culture if I am not an artist? This is where positionality comes into play. Positionality is often discussed in the literature on qualitative research methodologies and refers to the relationship between the researcher and the communities being studied (Bourke, 2014; Muhammad et al., 2015). Positionality is equally important to the teaching process because it involves ongoing self-analysis (Bourke, 2014). Leitch and Day (2000) argue for a reflective practice that helps link personal and professional identities in the classroom which Kerber (2013) suggests leads to authenticity through teaching. Cousin (2010) offers the notion of positional reflexivity. From this perspective, my identity is seen as important to the teaching and learning process because it affects relationships within the classroom setting but also what I am able to do within the academy. I have inherited privilege in the academy because of my race, but lack privilege in other areas because of my gender. I have a shared biography with my students because teaching and learning are inhabited and shaped by both the educator and students' identities.

I am keenly aware of the dilemmas raised by Gosa and Fields (2012) and am primarily concerned here with the question of expertise and authority, and hip-hop based education as cultural theft and misappropriation. I do not claim to be an expert on hip-hop and as Gosa and Fields (2012) suggest, hip-hop has its own cultural capital and White educators might lack the authenticity associated with it. For the most part, academia is often separate from what happens in communities; however, my work as a public sociologist allows me to navigate these two spheres and build a bridge between them. I essentially have an insider/outside identity (Bourke, 2014). My academic position is special in the communities that I work with, especially among youth in juvenile detention centers who may not know many college professors. I step out of the academy and work side-by-side with community organizers, advocates, artists, and many others. I am most often referred to as "Doc" even though I ask to be called by "Andrea" and introduced as "that college professor." My position within the academy grants me privileges to do this work, and with it, comes a certain level of social responsibility to address the politics of identity (i.e., my identity, the identities of my students, the identities of artists, and the larger identities of the communities that I am embedded within). The Sociology of Hip-Hop Culture class is not possible as currently conceptualized without the support of artists and community members. Thus, I see it as vitally important to build mutually beneficial partnerships that create social and cultural capital in and out of the academy. This aligns with the principles of critical hip-hop pedagogy and allows me to create a classroom community full of authenticity that encourages social justice in higher education that can result in social justice through higher education (Kerber, 2013).

CONCLUSION

Where do we go from here? The Sociology of Hip-Hop Culture class continues to evolve with each iteration because of the changing social and political climate and the changing needs of students. Above all, the goal is still to create transformative and emancipatory possibilities through teaching and learning. Community collaborations are an essential part of achieving this goal. Critical hip-hop pedagogy provides a roadmap for doing so and a way for educators to reflect on their own power, identity, and positionality. Freire (1968/1970) so poignantly asserted that the oppressed could liberate themselves through education. We can assist with this endeavor by creating a classroom that legitimizes different forms of knowledge and ways of knowing. Hip-hop was built on this premise and continues to provide a space for intellectualism both in and out of the academy.

REFERENCES

Akom, A.A. (2009). Critical hip hop pedagogy as a form of liberatory praxis. *Equity & Excellence in Education, 42*(1), 52–66.

Astin, A.W., & Astin, H.S. (2006). Foreword. In A.W. Chickering, J.C. Dalton, & L. Stamm (Eds), *Encouraging authenticity and spirituality in higher education* (pp. vii–xi). San Francisco, CA: Jossey-Bass.

Bourke, B. (2014). Positionality: Reflecting on the research process. *The Qualitative Report, 19*(33), 1–9.

Cousin, G. (2010). Positioning positionality: The reflexive turn. In M. Savin-Baden & C. Howell Major (Eds.), *New approaches to qualitative research: Wisdom & uncertainty* (pp. 9–18). London, England: Routledge.

Elligan, D. (2000). Rap therapy: A culturally sensitive approach to psychotherapy with young African American men. *Journal of African American Men, 5*(3), 27–36.

Freire, P. (1970). *Pedagogy of the oppressed* (M. Bergman Ramos, Trans). New York, NY: Herder and Herder. (Original work published 1968)

Gosa, L.T., & Fields, G.T. (2012). Is hip-hop education another hustle? The (ir)responsible use of hip-hop as pedagogy. In B.J. Porfilio & M.J. Viola (Eds.), *Hip-Hop(e): The cultural practice and critical pedagogy of international hip-hop* (pp. 1–24). New York, NY: Peter Lang.

Hill, M. (2009). Scared straight: Hip-hop, outing, and the pedagogy of queerness. *The Review of Education, Pedagogy, and Cultural Studies, 31*, 29–54.

Irby, D.J., & Hall, H.B. (2011). Fresh faces, new places: Moving beyond teacher-researcher perspectives in hip-hop-based education research. *Urban Education, 46*(2), 216–240.

Jenkins, T. (2011). A beautiful mind: Black male intellectual identity and hip-hop culture. *Journal of Black Studies, 42*, 1231–1251.

Kobin, C., & Tyson, E. (2006). Thematic analysis of hip-hop music: Can hip-hop in therapy facilitate empathic connections when working with clients in urban settings? *The Arts in Psychotherapy, 33*, 343–356.

Kreber, C. (2013). *Authenticity in and through teaching in higher education*. London, England: Routledge.

Ladson-Billings, G. (1995). Toward a theory of culturally relevant pedagogy. *American Education Research Journal, 32*(3), 465–491.

Ladson-Billings, G. (2014). Culturally relevant pedagogy 2.0: Aka the remix. *Harvard Educational Review, 84*(1), 74–135.

Leitch, R., & Day, C. (2000). Action research and reflective practice: Towards a holistic view. *Educational Action Research, 8*(1), 179–193.

Love, B.L. (2015). What is hip-hop-based education doing in *nice* fields such as early childhood and elementary education? *Urban Education, 50*(1), 106–131.

Love, B.L. (2018). Knowledge reigns supreme: The fifth element, hip-hop critical pedagogy & community. In C. Emdin & E. Adjapong (Eds.), *#HipHopEd: The compilation on hip-hop education* (Vol. 1, pp. 38–43). Leiden, The Netherlands: Brill.

Muhammad, M., Wallerstein, N., Sussman, A.L., Avila, M., Belone, L., & Duran, B. (2015). Reflections on researcher identity and power: The impact of positionality on community based participatory research (CBPR) processes and outcomes. *Critical Sociology, 41*(7–8):1045–1063.

Palmer, P. (1998). *The courage to teach*. San Francisco, CA: Josey-Bass.

Paris, D., & Alim, H.S. (2014). What are we seeking to sustain through culturally sustaining pedagogy? A loving critique forward. *Harvard Educational Review, 84*(1), 85–100.

Petchauer, E. (2010). Sampling practices and social spaces: Exploring a hip-hop approach to higher education. *Journal of College Student Development, 51*(4), 359–372.

Petchauer, E. (2011). Knowing what's up and learning what you're not supposed to: Hip-hop collegians, higher education, and the limits of critical consciousness. *Journal of Black Studies, 42*(5), 768–790.

Petchauer, E. (2015). Starting with style: Toward a second wave of hip-hop education research and practice. *Urban Education, 50*(1), 78–105.

Prier, D., & Beachum, F. (2008). Conceptualizing a critical discourse around hip-hop culture and Black male youth in educational scholarship and research. *International Journal of Qualitative Studies in Education, 21*(5), 519–535.

Rodríguez, L.F. (2009). Dialoguing, cultural capital, and student engagement: Toward a hip hop pedagogy in the high school and university classroom. *Equity & Excellence in Education, 42*(1), 20–35.

Rose, T. (2008). *The hip hop wars: What we talk about when we talk about hip hop—and why it matters.* New York, NY: Basic Civitas Books.

Sulé, V.T. (2015). White privilege? The intersection of hip-hop and whiteness as a catalyst for cross-racial interaction among white males. *Equity & Excellence in Education, 48*(2), 212–226.

Wessel, R.D., & Wallaert, K.A. (2011). Student perceptions of the hip hop culture's influence in the undergraduate experience. *Journal of College Student Development, 52*(2), 167–179.

CHAPTER THREE

A Boogie Down Production

Hip Hop as Disruption and Transformation

ANDREW TORRES

INTRODUCTION

When my partner's family traveled from Australia and Sri Lanka to attend our wedding in New York City, they immediately wanted to visit New York's tourist attractions such as Times Square, the Brooklyn Bridge, and Central Park. While I understood their desire to visit tourist attractions that draw millions of people yearly, I wondered if they would be interested in visiting the Bronx. Knowing that many of my partner's cousins listened to hip-hop music I inquired if they would be interested in visiting the birthplace of hip-hop, and they were intrigued. One day, towards the end of the summer of 2016, we took a drive to 1520 Sedgwick Ave, the birthplace of hip-hop. While we didn't gain access into the building I showed them the windows of the recreation room where Cindy Campbell threw a back-to-school party, and who along with her brother Clive, better known as DJ Kool Herc, are credited with kick-starting the hip-hop movement. Growing up in the Bronx, I felt compelled to show the beauty of the neighborhood that raised me to my in-laws, understanding that they more than likely would've not visited the Bronx had I not suggested the idea, mainly due to negative stigmas, or grand narratives, often projected onto the Bronx from those who have never set foot in the borough (Solorzano & Yosso, 2002).

Using hip-hop as a humanizing pathway, I was able to convince my new family to experience New York City through my eyes, and I believe that this is what hip-hop is all about; providing a pathway to empathize with lived realities of groups of people who are often misrepresented, misunderstood, and silenced. Moreover, hip-hop, "tells stories from the margins, from the vantage that most elite Americans refuse to acknowledge" (Forell, 2006, p. 31), a vantage point that is often, "the representative voice of urban youth, since the genre was created by and for them" (Morrell & Duncan-Andrade, 2002, p. 88). Hip-hop isn't just a genre of music for me, it has reflected what I lived through daily since I was born. Hip-hop has informed my identity development while affirming that my existence is both desirable and meaningful.

This chapter is written using the method of *racial storytelling* that "illustrates how my racial encounters from the past situate themselves in the current moment" (Johnson, 2017, p. 4), in an effort to chronicle the influence of hip-hop throughout various periods of my life, specifically, how hip-hop has informed and transformed my identity development as a youth, my pedagogical style as an educator and my current research as a doctoral student. These stories are racial because mine, my family, and my friend's existence in the United States is racialized and, therefore, race cannot be separated from my lived reality. This chapter may be considered an exercise in praxis, or "reflection and action upon the world in order to transform it" (Freire, 2000, p. 54), where I aim to utilize these stories to reflect on my past to better inform my present as I envision and build my future. In sharing these stories, my purpose is the same as when I write a poem, it's for me; a radical act of self-love. But what I've learned in writing and performing as a spoken word artist is that what we write for ourselves is often reflected in those we perform for.

To begin, I provide anecdotes that describe my history with hip-hop from childhood through adolescence and beyond. The section to follow will detail how I employed hip-hop within my lessons during my tenure as an English Language Arts teacher for a public middle school in the South Bronx. Subsequently, I will discuss the centrality of hip-hop to my current work as a doctoral student and how I've been able to incorporate hip-hop as a theoretical framework and action-oriented practice that addresses issues that I've faced as an Afro-Boricua student in a predominantly white university. To further arguments of the efficacy of hip-hop in education, I will then discuss how hip-hop provides evidence of a form of power and wisdom that I argue only exists within those who have lived with and through racial/cultural and complex trauma (Van der Kolk, Roth, Pelcovitz, Sunday, & Spinazzola, 2005; Carter, 2007). This chapter will conclude with a vision statement of what schooling could look like if hip-hop were accepted as a valid framework for educating racially minoritized youth.

BACK IN THE DAY, WHEN I WAS YOUNG

Familia

My initial introduction to music began with the musician of our family Pop (my maternal grandfather). To the trombone of Willie Colon, the voice of Hector Lavoe, and the piano of Eddie Palmieri, Pop's heavy hands would clap against the rawhide skin of his Latin Percussion (LP) congas driving the heartbeat of the song. One of my first photos as an infant is of me sitting in front of Pop's LP bongos trying to mimic his movements. With the smile and sense of excitement in my face, you would think I was about to blast off through the ceiling. It was nestled within these fond memories that I realized why my initial attraction to a song is the beat. Considering the historical origins of hip-hop, and how it began with mixing the breakdown portions of disco records to create a new beat that b-girls and b-boys could breakdance to or MCs could rhyme over, the beat has always been pivotal to the unique nature of hip-hop as a means of disruption, (re)imagination, and transformation.

As I learned to walk, the beat of the music that my family listened to encouraged me to bounce around trying to mimic another familiar act that I constantly observed my relatives doing, dancing. My cousin, G, was known for popping and locking and being able to dance like Michael Jackson. Nothing intrigued me more than wanting to be able to move like my cousin and as I grew, I got better at reflecting the swag, or the embodiment of urbanized culture, that my cousin so effortlessly embodied.

Beginning with the beat of the music and moving into dancing, hip-hop not only acted as the connective tissue between generations within my family, but it also provided a way to navigate my lived reality with the understanding that there is a rhythm to life that we must learn to dance to.

Throughout my youth, I received lessons within my home that involved literacies often used, "in the family, community, or with regard to popular culture" (Hallman, 2009, p. 38). These points give credence to the notion that "children's learning begins long before they attend school" (Vygotsky, 1978, p. 84). One thing that I have learned as a student in my youth and now as an educator is that learning and development for youth in the Bronx flourishes in and out of school, but is often not given recognition until it is associated with academic success. Unfortunately, in many cases administrators and teachers who do not employ a culturally sustaining pedagogy (McCarty & Lee, 2014; Paris, 2012) and/or a pedagogy that acknowledges their reality, oftentimes make racially minoritized youth feel that they must, "divorce themselves from their culture in order to be academically successful" (Emdin, 2016, p. 13) The lessons from my family naturally sustained our culture while shaping my outlook on my everyday reality and influencing my development from a very young age. Even to this day, I can still hear Biggie coming from my uncle's room, echoing off the walls as I ran through the narrow hallway of my grandparents home.

Adolessons (Adolescence)

In the summer of 1999, my mother and stepfather moved my brother, sister and myself to Sanford, Florida. For four years, I was immersed in southern rural living where, with my slick back gelled hair, I was often essentialized as the Rico Suave kid from the Bronx. The schools I attended and the area where I lived in were predominantly Black and many of the youth that I came across never encountered a person of Puerto Rican descent. My peers were mainly interested in hearing me say *water* or *coffee*, because, according to them, New Yorkers have a funny accent. Living in the South, which has historically influenced the evolution of hip-hop, helped introduce me to artists such as Outkast, Ludacris, and T.I. I had a difficult time in Florida, mainly due to bullying I experienced in and out of school. To find a way to start building a reputation for myself, I started making mixtapes of popular hip-hop songs for young people who lived in the same apartment complex and went to the same school as me. I charged 5 dollars for each mixtape and as more young people heard about the mixtapes I started developing a reputation that garnered me some pretty amazing friends. In Sanford, anyone with a car always hooked up their sound systems to have huge subwoofers that emphasized deep bass, shaking the ground so you knew they were coming from a mile away. One day I remember hearing someone playing a mixtape I made on their car's sound system and the sense of belonging I felt in that moment as I watched my friends dance to the music. My passion for beats would translate to my grandparents buying me a drum set that I would play daily alongside my favorite hip-hop song, following in the footsteps of the musician of our family.

After four years in Florida, I returned to the Bronx and while in high school, I spent much of my time playing basketball with my friends and participating in extracurricular activities that were rooted in hip-hop. One such activity was joining an after-school DJing group that inspired me to get my own DJ set. Spinning and scratching vinyl became a source of fun and camaraderie amongst my group of friends. We would freestyle to instrumentals and this lyrical practice would carry over into the school space. These freestyles would form in school, driving to a basketball game, or walking to the bus stop after school—anywhere and everywhere. Another frequent hobby while in school was making beats anywhere physically possible like classroom desks, lockers, lunch tables, clapping our hands in a rhythm, and beatboxing. During my high school prom, there was a point where a dance battle took form on the dance floor, reminiscent of breakdancing battles that have been a cornerstone of hip-hop culture since its inception. Hip-hop was central to my high school experience, especially considering that my beginnings with spoken word began during my sophomore year when I joined an after-school poets society. From practicing ways to perform better in a cypher, or a circle, to the way that we hyped each other up during performances to build our confidence, hip-hop defined the culture of our after-school space. The open mics and slams that I began performing at would often have a DJ playing hip-hop music to set the mood and experiencing artists performing various forms of art on stage, including hip-hop songs, has given me confidence in my public speaking skills and in creating humanizing connections across lines of difference with youth from all five boroughs. As Denise Taliaferro Baszile (2009) explains, "today, hip hop lives on in multifarious representations, including socially conscious rap, gangsta rap, R&B sampling, spoken word, clothing (Rockawear, FUBU, etc.)" (p. 6). My wardrobe consisted of hip-hop brands such as Ecko Unltd. and Sean John, my kicks, a colloquial term for sneakers, were always Nike or Adidas, and 90% of the music on my MP3 player was hip-hop. Stuart Hall (1983) puts it succinctly, "hip hop was one of the first cultural sites where we discover and play with the identifications of ourselves, where we are imagined, where we are represented, not only to the audiences out there who do not get the message but to ourselves for the first time" (p. 470). During my formative years, hip-hop was an incredibly salient part of my identity that continues to shape who I am as an adult.

Adulthood

Upon entering college at a State University of New York (SUNY), dubstep had become a popular genre of music. Knowing my love of beats, I was immediately drawn to the hip-hop styled rhythms that were layered with electronic synths and vocals. Throughout college, I would often find myself attending parties and events where the majority in attendance ethnically and culturally identified as Black, Latinx, and Afro-Caribbean and where the primary music selection was hip-hop, Caribbean and/or Latinx music. Even moving three and a half hour away from the Bronx, I found myself drawn to the same culture that raised me. I found myself joining dance groups such as Quimbamba, a dance group that would perform routines that mixed African, Caribbean, Bachata, Salsa, and hip-hop music and moves. This experience brought back memories of the feeling that dancing gave me when I was a child watching my family. While an undergrad, I vividly remember listening to J. Coles *The Warm Up* (2009) and *The Come Up* (2007) mixtapes. Listening to an artist who attended and graduated from a college in New York rap about his experiences as an undergraduate student made me feel less displaced as a racially minoritized student at a predominantly white university. Toward my senior year, a shift occurred in my spoken word writing as I listened to Kendrick Lamar's *Overly Dedicated (O.D.)* (2010) and *Section 80* (2011) mixtapes. Kendrick's use of alliteration in *Ignorance is Bliss* when he said, "cats so watered down clowns can sing Titanic/Tie titanium around their neck and watch 'em panic," heavily influenced how I began constructing the wordplay in my poems. I couldn't escape the relevancy of their songs knowing that I wasn't too far from them in age or experience, which is how I imagine my mom, my uncles, and my cousins must have felt growing up listening to hip-hop artists that they resonated with.

Another instance of how hip-hop has continued to influence me through adulthood was during my partner and I's wedding. During a portion of the reception, I surprised my partner with a dance routine that one of my best friends' helped me come up with over the span of two weeks. Within the routine, we combined a variety of popular hip-hop dances including the Milly Rock and Hit Dem Folks dances. Even now, as a father to an incredibly intuitive, intelligent, courageous and beautiful little baby girl, I find myself beatboxing and dancing with her to the likes of Lauryn Hill and Nas. Hip-hop has also become more acceptable in schools and classrooms where it is used as a site of sociocultural exploration, which can be understood as, "the study of Hip Hop culture, music, and elements, alongside an examination of issues within one's surroundings to create positive change in one's community" (Love, 2013, p. 8). The way that I used hip-hop to create positive change in my community was as a culturally relevant/sustaining pedagogical tool as an English Language Arts teacher.

BRING THE STREETS INTO THE CLASSROOM

One common mantra of educators that I have experienced is "when you step into my classroom, leave the streets outside." This often reflects a tension between the teacher and students that is rooted in majoritarian "stories that carry layers of assumptions that persons in positions of racialized privilege bring with them to discussions of racism, sexism, classism, and other forms of subordination" (Solorzano & Yosso, 2002, p. 28). Knowing that there weren't many teachers who looked like and came from the same communities as their students, I sought to shift students' perceptions of what it means to come from the Bronx. My goal as an educator of color was to disrupt this outdated ideology that perceives the "streets" in terms that seek to frame our communities as damaged (Tuck, 2009). I also attempted to show the inherent forms of desirability that exist within the students and our community, which is specifically, "concerned with understanding complexity, contradiction, and the self-determination of lived lives" (2009, p. 416). To this end, I reversed the pedagogical standpoints that many teachers honed over their years in the classroom and invited students to bring their lived realities into the classroom as a means of informing and developing our everyday lessons, rather than coming into the classroom claiming to have the keys to lifelong success.

Using hip-hop as a pedagogical tool, I invited students to listen to the Biggie Smalls song, *Juicy* and to compare the imagery of the lyrics to the images shown in the video as their first homework assignment for the year. The goal of this assignment was to see which literary modality captured the essence of Biggie's lived reality more, the words or the video. After assigning the homework, a student named Ani seemed anxious and I couldn't figure out why. I assumed that this assignment was low impact, an exercise in critical literacy, and a creative way of addressing state-mandated literacy skills that students were required to master within the seventh grade. Ani came to my desk after class and asked if she could have an alternative assignment because her father was strict and wouldn't allow her to listen to hip-hop music, as it was considered a negative influence in her family. She informed me that she wanted to do well in the class, but was afraid of getting in trouble with her father. I asked if she would be comfortable listening to any song that her father deems appropriate and to do the same comparison of lyrics and music video. Relieved, she said, "I think I can do that." The next day, Ani came up to me and handed me her assignment with an excited expression on her face. Before I could read her homework assignment, she shyly said, "Mr. Torres I have never heard Biggie Smalls before but I listened to the song you assigned (unbeknownst to her father) and I couldn't stop listening." She went on to explain how she listened to different songs by Biggie for a couple of hours and how she was hooked. There was a sense of liberation in listening to Biggie that many of the students that I worked with did not expect on their first day of English Language Arts.

Hip-hop is an integral part of my pedagogy and many of the activities that were done in class, especially those on spoken word, focused on breaking down the lyrics to hip-hop songs and discussing their connections and saliency to the lived realities of the students. During these moments, students would often say how our class "didn't feel like a regular classroom" and that our lessons engaged them in ways that made learning something that couldn't be contained in a classroom; they learned to read and write their world (Freire & Macedo, 1987). One such activity was dissecting the lyrics of Kanye West's song *All Falls Down* for his use of various literary devices including symbolic language, simile, metaphor, and rhyme scheme. Students enjoyed going over the lyrics in class and would rap along every time we watched the music video to compare different modalities of cultural expression. Students were also allowed to listen to music during writing time and there would often be hip-hop music blaring from my computer speakers during my lunch break and preparation periods. In all, hip-hop provided a humanizing pathway toward complexifying and exploring our lived realities through analysis and discussion of hip-hop song lyrics. As we investigated the lived realities of hip-hop artists as expressed through their lyrics, we also explored ourselves and deepened our understanding of what learning and education could look like. Unfortunately, the administration did not like how I taught and found it to be a form of subordination because I would never use the scripted curriculum that was assigned to me. By my second year of teaching, I was constantly surveilled—administrators asking for all of my unit and lesson plans ahead of me teaching them so that they could vet the lessons and decide if they were appropriate for the young people I taught. It was around December of 2015 when I was told by the principal of the school at a disciplinary meeting, "If you want to continue teaching this way, you either need to go teach in a high school or start your own school." As soon as I left their office, I applied for a doctoral program and decided that I would start a school that is funded and built from the ground up by, for, and with/alongside the people of the Bronx.

FROM THE BOOGIE DOWN TO THE IVIES

Never in a million years would I have guessed that I would enroll in a doctoral program. When I finalized my transition from teaching to being a full-time graduate student I felt frustrated that I wasn't able to navigate some of the hardships of being a teacher and fell into the category of teaching for two years and leaving. All I knew was that I had the energy and privilege to make moves that I would intentionally use to give back to my community in sustainable, authentic, humanizing, and decolonizing ways. Hip-hop can be described as a form of disruption in many contexts including the disruption of conventional ways of wearing kicks, such as when Run-DMC wore their shell toes without laces in their *My Adidas* music video. This notion of disruption is at the foundation of how I navigate the academy now as an Afro-Boricua parent-scholar. Much of what I've learned about research inquiry—whether qualitative or quantitative, whether data collection or analysis—is how it has historically reflected a system of control. This system of control seeks to designate what is credited with being valid in regards to knowledge production and meaning making. Oftentimes these definitions are developed by cisgender, white men who act as gatekeepers within the academies. Within my own research, I have sought to disrupt this historical pattern of dehumanizing research. Researchers often colonize culture by invading cultural forms of knowledge production and rendering them irrelevant while reaping the glory of studying their exoticism. What often occurs is a sense that racially minoritized folks, who are historically excluded from academia, are not meant to be within these spaces as scholars, otherwise known as imposter syndrome.

Although it hurts to be away from the Bronx, I have volunteered my time and efforts to a community in the New England area that shares many socioeconomic, sociocultural, and racial similarities to the Bronx. Currently, the research study that is underway focuses on exploring the various ways that embodied arts—a reconceptualization of performance arts that aims to center the dialectical relationship between the body, mind, and soul that occurs in the production and performance of works of art—might address racial/cultural and complex trauma (Carter, 2007; Van der Kolk et al., 2005). Participants and I are conceptualizing trauma as a perpetual haunting of physical, emotional, spiritual, and mental violence that goes beyond a singular event or crisis; a haunting that is both lived with and lived through (Craps, 2013; Johnson, 2017). All participants will have a say in the data collection, analysis, and write up stages of the research study, including how they wish to be addressed within write-ups, which will ensure that their voice is not misrepresented and can be considered as a way of decolonizing the research process by centering participants as experts in the topic being studied. I have also invited participants to consider co-writing pieces that we can later publish, in addition to attending conferences to present on the work together rather than me presenting on their behalf. It is in this context that I aim to build a project in humanization because "if we can see our participants as those who are in the process of constructing knowledge with us rather than as separate from us, we break down the artificial boundaries or binaries of researcher/subject that have been building over time" (Kinloch & San Pedro, 2014, p. 32). Breaking down these binaries is another variation of disruption that challenges traditional frameworks of research inquiry. Hip-hop is about validating lived realities and language forms by disrupting majoritarian narratives that are being told about our communities, and the study we are building aims to do the same. Many fans of hip-hop listen as a way to understand the culture of the hood (inner-city, urbanized communities), to a certain extent, our research project will help scholars and educators in academia understand the hood in ways that are authentic to those of us who were raised and live in the hood. By speaking our truth into existence and telling our uncensored stories we become the gatekeepers of our culture and community choosing who we invite into our worlds. These stories are often missing or suppressed within scholarship, the same as they were from mainstream music when hip-hop was born, and we seek to shift this issue by considering embodied arts as a modality of racial storytelling that, "allows us to confront our racial hauntings and to work against our own miseducation while moving toward liberation and self-actualization" (Johnson, 2017, p. 4). Embodied arts as a modality of racial storytelling invites us to center our lived realities in transparent, authentic, and vulnerable ways that are meaningful to us, in order to engender a deeper sense of belonging amongst members of racially minoritized and urbanized communities.

THE POWER OF STREET WISDOM

Academic knowledge is often championed as the type of knowledge that is necessary for success in our society, which often marginalizes any alternative form of knowledge that may exist, such as street smarts. Our body, mind, and soul shape and are shaped by our lived realities, therefore we must understand what forms of knowledge production and meaning making emerge from our experiences. Despite majoritarian narratives that view our communities in damaged terms, we hold our communities in high esteem because we care about our communities and therefore a new dialogue to engender a paradigm shift in how our communities are viewed as necessary. Using embodied arts as a modality of racial storytelling, educators and scholars can invite the various forms of knowledge production and meaning making that racially minoritized youth already possess into academic spaces and scholarship. Educators modeling transparency and vulnerability, by sharing stories that reflect their own lived realities, promote trusting, deep, and meaningfully authentic relationships that help to engender a sense of solidarity between them and students. We as educators, should not fear criticism, feedback, or ideas from students and should be more open to creating inclusive opportunities to work alongside young people in developing our daily lessons. In this way, we are disrupting and challenging traditional conceptualizations of the student/teacher relationship through the use of organic, or naturally developing/growing with young people, methods that resist forms of control in education.

Gentrification, another system of control, is nothing new and the Bronx is not immune to its symptoms, but after being introduced to local small business owners, I have personally encountered the growing network of individuals who are fighting to keep the changes that are occurring in the Bronx informed by the people of the Bronx and their needs. This reflects the spirit of hip-hop that continues to thrive in its birthplace; a refusal to back down and a disruption of whiteness. In other boroughs, these changes are often associated with privilege and whiteness, where commercial and residential buildings are bought by outside stakeholders aiming to bring in more revenue and increase the standard of living at the expense of displacing thousands of folks who have lived in these communities for generations. This only happens in communities that are labeled as damaged or deemed in need of modernization. Rarely does this process include the voices or consider the lived realities of those who already reside there—perpetuating settler colonialism and its legacy of stealing land, erasure, and displacement (Tuck, 2009).

Hip-hop is an incredibly powerful and salient pathway toward understanding lived realities that are often misrepresented. Through the use of racial storytelling that, "requires us to revisit memories that we hope to forget but that continue to live on—memories that trigger feelings of joy, guilt, happiness, sadness, frustration, anger, and rage" (Johnson, 2017, p. 6), I have aimed to show how hip-hop has grounded itself throughout various stages of my upbringing, to my pedagogical stance as an English Language Arts teacher, and now as a parent-scholar of color. Hip-hop belongs in schools because I and people like me belong in schools. Hip-hop is innovative because the people who started it and the people who keep it alive are innovative as we navigate our lived realities. Hip-hop provides proof that we are not broken, that we have always been and continue to be a community of the powerful and wise. Now is the time to show it by bringing the voices of our communities to the forefront of research inquiry and education reform.

REFERENCES

Baszile, D.T. (2009). Deal with It We Must: Education, Social Justice, and the Curriculum of Hip Hop Culture. *Equity & Excellence In Education, 42*(1), 6–19.

Carter, R.T. (2007). Racism and psychological and emotional injury: Recognizing and assessing race-based traumatic stress. *The Counseling Psychologist, 35*(1), 13–105.

Craps, S. (2013). *Postcolonial witnessing : Trauma out of bounds.* New York : Palgrave Macmillan

Emdin, C. (2016). *For white folks who teach in the hood ... and the rest of y'all too: Reality pedagogy and urban education.* New York, NY: Beacon Press.

Forell, K.L.H. (2006). Ideas in practice: Bringin' hip-hop to the basics. *Journal Of Developmental Education, 30*(2), 28–33.

Freire, P., & Macedo, D. (1987). *Reading the word and the world.* Westport, CT: Bergin & Garvey.

Freire, P. (2000). *Pedagogy of the oppressed* (p. 72). New York, NY: Continuum.

Hall, S. (1983). What is this "black" in black popular culture? In M. Wallace (Ed.), *Black popular culture.* New York, NY: Beacon Press.

Hallman, H.L. (2009). "Dear Tupac, you speak to me": Recruiting hip hop as curriculum at a school for pregnant and parenting teens. *Equity & Excellence In Education, 42*(1), 36–51.

Johnson, L.L. (2017). The racial hauntings of one Black male professor and the disturbance of the self (ves): Self-actualization and racial storytelling as pedagogical practices. *Journal of Literacy Research, 49*(4), 476–502.

Kinloch, V., & San Pedro, T. (2014). The space between listening and storying: Foundations for projects in humanization. In D. Paris & M.T. Winn (Eds.), *Humanizing research: Decolonizing qualitative inquiry with youth and communities* (pp. 21–42). Thousand Oaks, CA: Sage.

Love, B.L. (2013). Oh, they're sending a bad message. *International Journal Of Critical Pedagogy, 4*(3), 24–39.

McCarty, T., & Lee, T. (2014). Critical culturally sustaining/revitalizing pedagogy and Indigenous education sovereignty. *Harvard Educational Review, 84*(1), 101–124.

Morrell, E., & Duncan-Andrade, J. (2002). Promoting academic literacy with urban youth through engaging hip-hop culture. *The English Journal, 91*(6), 88–92.

Paris, D. (2012). Culturally sustaining pedagogy: A needed change in stance, terminology, and practice. *Educational Researcher, 41*(3), 93–97.

Solórzano, D.G., & Yosso, T.J. (2002). Critical race methodology: Counter-storytelling as an analytical framework for education research. *Qualitative inquiry, 8*(1), 23–44.

Tuck, E. (2009). Suspending damage: A letter to communities. *Harvard Educational Review, 79*(3), 409–428.

Van der Kolk, B.A., Roth, S., Pelcovitz, D., Sunday, S., & Spinazzola, J. (2005). Disorders of extreme stress: The empirical foundation of a complex adaptation to trauma. *Journal of Traumatic Stress: Official Publication of The International Society for Traumatic Stress Studies, 18*(5), 389–399.

Vygotsky, L.S., & Cole, M. (1978). *Mind in society: The development of higher psychological processes.* Cambridge: Harvard University Press.

CHAPTER FOUR

More than Beats, More than Rhymes, More than Life

The Life of Hip-Hop and Its Developing Identity

NAPOLEON WELLS
Clafin University
@NapoleonBXSith

Hip-hop, from its birth, and along all stages of its development, has been regarded as equal parts ethereal and ephemeral. It has been dismissed as little more than a cultural and musical fad, struggled toward becoming a human artistic force, and time and again been pressed to address the question of "who am I" for those whose voice the life of hip-hop projects. Sanctuaries as alive and thriving as high school cafeterias and grand arenas have been packed and erected for the worship of the beatsmith and rhymesayer. Battles have been waged in the pit of the cypher. Hip-Hop, the world over, has developed many sounds, identities, and languages (Morgan & Bennett, 2011). Year over year, as hip-hop has grown, morphed, regressed, progressed, struggled, cried out, affirmed and lived with the question of "*who am I?*"

While there should be no doubt that hip-hop has lived a great many existences, shaped by those who engage and build it, it began its life as an instrument. It was first a tool of expression. It lived its early life, from the joyful hubris of the Sugar Hill Gang's "Rapper's Delight" to the traumatic journal entry of "The Message" by Grandmaster Flash and the Furious Five, as a means of giving the poor and disenfranchised an outlet for projecting their lives up and out.

Here, with hip-hop, was the natural extension of the arts and acts of the Civil Rights era, reborn, after they had given way to the expression of Black life portrayed stereotypically through Blaxploitation films (Aldridge, 2005). The writings, art, and activism of that era relegated to text, archive, and memory. After the lull of the sun setting on the Civil Rights era, came another means for combating oppressive erasure, born of the poor, disenfranchised, and continually oppressed. Hip-hop became a weapon formed of the few experiential scraps trickled down into urban centers, and fueled by the African diasporic and continental spirits and energies that sustained the families and children that would go on to nurture hip-hop. The question of identity development has been explored as it relates to fundamental parts of the human condition including sexuality (Bilodeau & Renn, 2005), race/culture/ethnicity (Cross, 1971; Helms, 1990) and even as hip-hop has as a cultural, emotional and musical force has influenced identity development (Hill, 2009).

As a lifelong fan of hip-hop and its culture, and as an observer of said culture and trained Psychologist, I have long studied the growth, influence, and development of that culture. Through this dual lens of fan and Psychologist, I have considered the ways in which the same socioeconomic factors which would impact the overall development of a single being, would then impact hip-hop, as a being. Further, I have questioned how these factors which influence identity development in individuals, would impact identity development in the culture of hip-hop.

African American and Latino/Latinx communities, those influential in the development of hip-hop culture, have historically faced challenges with regard to healthy identity development. From the conflict which arises from having often competing racial, national and ethnic identities (Hughes et al., 2015), to the racist oppression of self-identity and expression (Papish, 2015), and psychologically toxic depictions of Black and Latino/Latinx identity development in media (Barnett & Flynn, 2014; Bender, 2003), these communities have confronted many avenues of resistance when seeking to define themselves in the American context.

Considering this history and these factors, I propose a model for identity development, rooted in an understanding of the growth of hip-hop, as influenced by its historical and cultural contexts. It is my assertion that, as hip-hop served to challenge cultural norms, it served as a model for urban identity development counter to the various societal influences which toxically impacted the Black and Brown communities which fed hip-hop. As with other identity development models, I propose the development of identity stages rooted in the developmental history of hip-hop and its existence.

As stated, a number of emotional/cognitive identity development models propose that identity develops in stages (Gay, 1985; McDermott & Samson, 2005; Yip, Sellers, & Seaton, 2006). Most existing models suggest that identity develops through process and experience. There is the idea that milestones, environment, and socialization meet to impact development. Next, most models suggest that identity is fundamentally fluid, allowing living beings to move to and through identity stages in no clearly defined order. Individuals then regress and progress as they and their appraisals of their circumstances necessarily shift and change. Within these models, identity, when tethered to the human condition, is never a single thing.

Identity development models typically identify the various stages by their marked characteristics, behaviors, attitudes, and traits. Often, these are marked by developmental hurdles or crises. Considering the oppressive, segregationist, racist and classist forces that produced the conditions, which birthed hip-hop culture, a model for identity development in hip-hop, is not only possible but essential for the community to understand and process itself as a full, realized being.

THE STAGES OF HIP-HOP THROUGH IDENTITY DEVELOPMENT

In examining hip-hop as a true, living, conscious and growing "being," we should examine the development of hip-hop across its lifespan, complete with necessary emotional and social influences, milestones, traumas, and critical periods which have fed its evolution. To that end, I propose a model of hip-hop identity development including five major stages (Mic Check/Pre-Encounter, Fight the Power/ Encounter, Idol Worship/Immersion-Emersion, The Great Migration/Internalization, Coping/Commitment), tied to periods of time, critical artistic works, and cultural shifts in the overall community which, at all times, has ultimately fed, stabilized and shaped hip-hop as a living entity.

In outlining these stages, I will identify unique influences, sketch a rough time frame for the development of that stage, describe the social and emotional factors which impacted hip-hop's developing sense of self in that stage. Then, where appropriate, I will draw links at junctions where one stage directly overlaps or tethers to other stages. Also, consider the influence of person and concept here, reciprocal. Hip-hop is a living thing, fed by the community of minds and practitioners who live with it, as the people are fed, ministered to and partake of hip-hop.

To discuss this development, I will link Hip-hop's core stages to Cross' (1991) five critical Black Identity development stages, with a Hip-Hop identifier for each. In each stage, I will refer to hip-hop as a "being," focusing on its development as a growing organism, personifying its character and personality traits, and tying these to its overall identity. As hip-hop will be discussed as a being, I will reference the impact that experience and growth have had on hip-hop, including any symptoms at a given stage that would be consistent with emotional struggles or disorders. Of note, these inferences regarding the development of hip hop overtime are first hand and intimately tied to my love for the culture and witnessing of these changes. Also, much like the overlap in identity development, there will be overlap in the periods of time reflected in each of these stages.

STAGE 1: MIC CHECK/PRE-ENCOUNTER (1976–1985)

In his Pre-Encounter stage, Cross (1971) describes a being largely identified and having absorbed the belief system of the dominant culture. In the context of both Black racial identity and the identity of hip-hop, that culture would be White and American. He goes on to indicate that the being, in this stage, is largely unaware of the implications of race on their own lives.

The mid to late 1970s proved to be most challenging for urban communities of color, all over the United States. Where there was the widespread hope born of the activism and creativity of the Civil Rights Era, the 1970s saw a return to those same communities battling growing poverty and erasure. Voices, organic within the community, and artistic, dedicated to affirmation and revolution and progress, had either been violently silenced or replaced culturally, often by other art forms and creators.

In urban Black America, the decade of the 1970s had the feel of a mind settling in, closing its shutters and making efforts to recover from the period of trauma visited by much of the 1960s. Where the 1960s began with struggle, loud proclamations, and asserting personhood, demonstrated, in part, by the voices of resistance which became prominent on the world stage, there was still the reality of home. In a five year window from 1963–1968, the movement toward equal and civil rights lost Medgar Evers, Malcolm X, and Martin Luther King Jr., all to assassinations. The dissolution and waning political, psychic and popular influence of the Black Panther Party, and other influential urban and community organizations also contributed to a strain of malaise and apathy not seen during the Civil Rights era of the 1960s (Lehman, 2006). There was, in the largely crumbling infrastructures of urban centers, a kind of spiritual, emotional and artistic hangover.

The rush and urgency of Black artistry of the prior 20 years lost much of its social and world influence. Jazz music became greater on the world stage than in its native land, rhythm and blues was identified almost entirely with urban radio and urban audiences, with crossover acts finding their influence diminished in the 1970s. Black musicians thrived in Funk and crossed over into other more popular musical forms, often without the revolutionary voice common in the Civil Rights era (Mahon, 2000; Morant, 2011). Black American cinema of the time belonged to the era of Blaxploitation films (Quinn, 2010; Lott, 1991). These typically being hyper-violent, often misogynist, focused on "real" urban decay, and while often empowering with regard to crafting new Black identity archetypes, treated as relatively disposable.

The outlook of the South Bronx of the late 1970s was bleak, representing one of the poorest voting districts in the United States, remaining so this day, with over 31 percent of its residents living below the poverty line, per census data (www.census.gov/SAIPE). The neighborhoods were scarred by burned out, abandoned buildings, failing schools, and rampant gang activity.

The resistance music and art of the Civil Rights era had been pushed to cultural margins, with disco and more popular singing/dancing musical groups assuming positions of prominence in the 1970s. Resistance music, culturally, became the purview of the spoken word artist, with the late 1960s and early 1970s giving rise to The Last Poets and Gil Scott-Heron (Hamilton, 2011). The literal precursor to formal rap music, these resistance artists use African drum, jazz, blues, and all available forms to produce their sound. The spoken wordsmith, the lyricist, began to be seen as a critical musical and thought instrument (Scott, 2005). Like all of its musical ancestors, hip-hop, as genre music and culture, was born of ingenuity and necessity. Word and sound smiths competed in the parks, using whatever creative canvasses and spaces were available to them. Writing their names and scribing identities on any available surface. Crafting a symbol and sound of the body. Hip-hop was a tool, even without its community realizing it, in that space.

In this first identity development stage, at its inception, hip-hop is shouting, in all four of its early mediums, "I am here." Those four artistic and cultural mediums (rapping, breakdancing, graffiti art, and djing) came to be known as the "four elements" of hip-hop. In this stage, the body and mind of hip-hop are using the loudest and clearest possible sounds to shout an alarm, to commiserate, to draw attention, and to make of its shared consciousness and many souls, a monument. This stage was closest to Cross's (1971) pre-encounter stage. In this stage of Black identity development, Black people are receiving cues about what it means to be Black from their environment, broader, dominant White culture, and are only beginning to take steps toward defining their racial identity for themselves. The Mic Check/Pre-Encounter stage as it relates to the being of hip-hop, finds a being not fully identifying, but doing. There were the activities of rapping, break dancing, crafting graffiti and djing, but there was not yet a concerted effort for hip-hop, the being, to assert itself as a culture. While there were all of the trappings of culture, including fashion, customs, and language, hip-hop believed, as many did, that it would be little more than a developmental phase.

In this first stage, hip-hop is still well and truly living through the trauma of the growth and cresting of the Civil Rights Era. Ostensibly, the community of minds and souls which birthed hip-hop were reporting the symptoms of Posttraumatic Stress Disorder (PTSD) inherent in the illness. It was Grandmaster Flash who first outlined these in his seminal first verse on the song, "The Message." He reported severe hypervigilance, avoidance behaviors, irritability, depressed mood, and anhedonia. Hip-Hop as a being is struggling, in this stage, but is also finding the voice to journal, report, and process that struggle. If we are to examine the inception of hip-hop, we should consider that, as a being, it looked up and around and saw very little hope in its circumstances, but vitality in the people. Hip-Hop witnessed, daily, Black and Brown families making use of the few resources trickled down to them, and creating and sustaining lives. It is this mix, this alchemy, which lends itself to the psychology of Hip-Hop in that day. In these spaces, DJs sampled soul, disco and funk records to craft and mesh new sounds. Street lights were appropriated for power strips. Local parks became impromptu concert venues for Emcee battles. Night clubs, recreation centers, and street corners became impromptu coliseums for breakdancing battles. Akin to Cross's (1971) pre-encounter stage, the Mic Check stage of hip-hop's life sees it existing and doing, but not meditating intently on its own identity.

Inherent in that early sound, and early life is the demand of Hip-Hop that its body and mind be fully realized, fully functioning and fully dimensional. Where Grandmaster Flash and The Furious Five were essentially war reporters, the Sugarhill Gang were party promoters. There, in those early stages, during those first unsure steps, was Hip-Hop already trying on varying identity masks. It is in this first stage where hip-hop is not only aware and mindful of its abilities and struggles, but it is also asserting its voice, right to existence, and personhood. Here, hip-hop as a being was a tool for those truly forgotten. It provided those who were subjected to failing schools and denied the safety of the suburbs, a conduit to telling their story in their way. Hip-hop, in this first stage of identity development, shouted out its pain, affirmed its refusal to simply wither and die, and signaled a cultural and emotional call to arms for the community which birthed it. Key in this first stage is the development of a living, breathing sense of self. One unsure, and unsteady, but bold and exuberant, nonetheless. This first stage of identity development, the Mic Check, was a cry for help and self-care. The lyrics spoke to the direct experiences of poverty, and anguish, and hope and hubris, all motivated by spaces and dynamics of hip-hop's home.

In this stage, Mic Check/pre-encounter, you could see Hip-Hop trying on its many identity hats, seeing which felt best for which occasion, any and all, and giving these many points of view to the world all at once. This stage lived with the thoughtful, contemplative, street science ushered in by KRS-One and the Boogie Down Productions. In this very same developmental space, hip-hop lived with the youthful, playful exuberance of DJ Jazzy Jeff and the Fresh Prince. Love, maturation, and relationships were explored by Whodini, while artists like LL Cool J demonstrated the demands of balancing being both vulnerable and aggressive in hip-hop's early home. There was a struggle, but no true self-consciousness, no putting on of airs or censoring. Here, in Hip-Hop, was a child learning to speak up for itself for the first time, but having a trauma and life history which gave this voice a gravity, and desperation, and vitality.

STAGE 2: FIGHT THE POWER/ENCOUNTER (1986–1993)

Living beings are impacted by their context, overall environment, and exposure, in every stage of development. In his Encounter stage, Cross (1971, 1991) indicates that racial identity development is activated by a seminal event, or series of events, that bring about a confrontation with the existence, and impact of, racism in a being's life. There is a growing realization of what one has access to and is often denied, as a result of being Black. In this stage, the events which impact development and growth are often the result of experiences with White counterparts, White society, and contact with the dominant culture's norms.

Similarly, hip-hop as a being in this stage is now experiencing greater contact with the broader, majority society. There was a greater demand for hip-hop to make itself accessible to foreign neighbors, to travel, market and sell itself, and to become a growing part of the American cultural, artistic and musical fabric. This growth coincided directly with a growing White youth interest and consumption of hip-hop. Hip-hop was further absorbed into cultures the world over (Aidi, 2011; Cornyetz, 1994). While hip-hop was multi-layered and had diverse components (dance, fashion, beatboxing), it was the music and the Emcee which were most palatable. This simultaneous acceptance/rejection could mark the beginning of the Fight the Power/Encounter stage. Hip-Hop as a being was made to realize that it was being defined, in part, by others. Hip-Hop as a being was made to realize that its "value" was dictated to by others. In this stage, hip-hop was confronted with having to promote parts of its cultural self, while diminishing others, for the sake of satisfying a broader audience. While hip-hop was introduced with four core elements, what appeared to be engaged most was the music. Rap music popularly became "hip-hop" while the art forms of djing, breakdancing and graffiti art, became more niche.

By the mid-1980s, MTV, and growing cable television were bringing not only the sound, but sight of music, and the life that produced the music and musician, into living rooms all over the country. Hip-hop music and culture, its living breathing life and ways, were being shared with middle America. Its reach was beginning to be felt outside of the borders of the United States. The demand for hip-hop grew wherever this impact was felt. The music and culture of the parks and playgrounds and project houses were now being demanded on college campuses and in small arenas, all over.

This demand brought hip-hop into contact with the larger, White community well outside of its cultural headquarters of the urban centers. The voice of hip-hop was initially judged to be too coarse, too combative and too Black. This appealed to young, rebellious White teens and adolescents, but threatened their parents and caretakers. Hip-Hop, like heavy metal before it, had become a kind of cultural battleground for the mind of young White America. This contact pressed Hip-Hop into the hands, minds, fantasies, and homes of White neighbors, who demanded more, and greater, access. The mid to late 1980s presented a proliferation of Hip-Hop fans of diverse backgrounds, coupled with a development of varied voices projecting out of the body of Hip-Hop, as well. California, with the entrance of

N.W.A., provided us with a glimpse of those same themes of poverty, trauma, gang life, and survival, that prior had only had an Eastern accent and patois. Still a child, but growing, slightly older, and more certain, Hip-Hop begins to emerge wherever the voices who identified with the being of hip-hop, lived. Hip-Hop had incorporated a megaphone and other tools necessary to project its voice and message to a growing audience.

The next major developmental identity milestone is reached around the early 1990s. Hip-Hop's childhood is characterized by music, art, and dance that is uniquely, and necessarily, personifying the sound and look of the neighborhoods that birthed it. The DJs, MCs, graffiti artists, B-boys and girls, style and, were all aware of now having a means for projecting their lives to the world. That being's life is still characterized by ongoing neglect, poverty, and struggle. The 1980s gave birth to the Crack epidemic, which ravaged Black and urban communities even further. Hip-Hop became not only music of resistance but a kind of psychological self-report and dairy. Years of living with PTSD symptoms had created a kind of "sickness savvy," where all of those bearing the weight of this generational trauma could discuss it with comfort, knowing and sharing all of the requisite signs and symptoms, free of judgment and stigma, over the beat.

Further development and contact would see hip-hop begin to live and grow in other urban centers. The culture, and this being made its way to California, Florida, and the Midwest. The body and mind grew and changed to accommodate its new and greater sense of self. As hip-hop was now effectively an adolescent, as this stage of identity development, it could start to play with concepts of being and personhood and could reflect on its tumultuous childhood and with more diverse experiences.

With a broader cultural vocabulary, Hip-hop began to visit some of its ancestries, and pulled in the sounds of jazz, and sounds and sights of African pride and resistance from the Civil Rights era, at the same time that it struggled with the impact of trauma as represented out on the West Coast, in gang culture. In the same developmental space, were artists like KRS-One and X-Clan fusing Black Power symbols and ethos into their sound and imagery, Digable Planets producing self-aware hip-hop over jazz beats and MC Eiht journaling about the perils of gang life. All at once, Hip-Hop was demonstrating growth, pain, versatility, and the shifting identity of one so young, and still learning. Hip-hop, in this stage, wanted to love itself and fight. Hip-hop, in this stage, wanted to party, be irresponsible, love, be loved, connect and escape. There was the jazz, social consciousness and pride fueled sound of A Tribe Called Quest, hood griots in Nas and Big Daddy Kane, the burgeoning, threatening impact of so-called West Coast gangsta rap, and the Hip-Hop carnival-like arrival of Two Live Crew. Hip-Hop was growing outward, placing roots wherever its body was found, and its utility was needed. Hip-Hop was demonstrating diversity and overlap in its identity development.

In this stage, hip-hop became American music. It developed into a cultural machine producing widely impactful artists, developing widely impactful works. The early 1990s gave rise to the Wu-Tang Clan, Tupac, Outkast, Snoop Dogg, and others. Where Hip-Hop had been along the margins in its prior stage of development, it was now reaching everywhere, while its body, was still largely confined to urban centers. Hope and trauma, all in the same cultural cycle.

In this second stage of identity development, Hip-Hop was showing signs of maturity, wellness, and all of the traits of a being in flux stuck somewhere between coltish youth and impending adulthood. Equally critical in this stage is the morphing of the voice of Hip-Hop to represent its true body. All of the elements of Hip-Hop have always been unisex, but it is true in this, the encounter stage, where we begin to see the impact of women artists, a segment which plays such an important role in leadership in Black and Brown homes and life, joining and influencing the chorus of sound. M.C. Lyte, Queen Latifah, Yo-Yo, Salt and Pepa, and others, all pushed the art and culture, and had diverse voices of their own, in doing so. Here, in the Fight the Power stage, it became clear that Hip-Hop continued to become more self-aware. Hip-hop became more mindful of how many broad and varied identities and spaces it could assume and occupy, and wished to push its own boundaries well past its comfort toward self-actualization.

This stage, Fight the Power, one of transition, is characterized by bursts of pride (A Tribe Called Quest), and affirmation (Queen Latifah), and excess (Two Live Crew). A Tribe Called Quest, combined conscious hip-hop with reverence of jazz and social justice in their sound. Queen Latifah merged the ideas of uplifting community with challenging misogyny in society and hip-hop, while Two Live Crew introduced a distinctly festive atmosphere and focus on sexual power. It is here, in this stage of identity development, that we begin to see significant identity complexity growing and living within hip-hop.

STAGE 3: IDOL WORSHIP/IMMERSION-EMERSION (1991–2002)

In Cross' (1971) Immersion/Emersion stage of Black racial identity development, a being now actively surrounds themselves with symbols affirming their identity. A being in this stage will actively seek to explore affirming parts of their history and culture with the support of their peers. It is in this era where hip-hop is truly introduced to everyone, everywhere, though it still remained a relative novelty as a being, in most settings. Now fully immersed in American culture and politics, hip-hop is commodified, but hip-hop as a being could still not be said to be understood. While present in the fabric of the overall society, hip-hop became a fixture in an ever more culturally and economically segregated America.

In this stage of its identity development, hip-hop is showing its own kind of cultural growth and personal acceptance. There is a confidence to hip-hop knowing itself to be the voice of its generation. It is more engaged than it has ever been and experiences the same emotional tumult as its homeland during this time. In this stage, we begin to see warring emotions and tribalism, as parts of the self of hip-hop begin to shout for attention and dominance. A kind of regional tribalism sets in (East/Bad Boy vs West/Death Row), with newer voices emerging in other parts of the nation (Outkast, Goodie Mob, Geto Boys) as well. Hip-Hop is affirming its place, crafting its image, using its lingo and creating its own international superstars (Biggie/Snoop/Tupac) and crafting iconic institutions such as The Source magazine, and albums. Hip-hop had reached a point in its development where it could now fully immerse itself in its own media, content, and could see representations of itself nearly anywhere it traveled.

Hip-hop, in this stage, has grown and left home—The Bronx. It is in arenas, on television, and in movies. It is using its voice to speak for itself, confidently, but it has left behind the era of true, profound self-love, and has moved toward excess. While boastful hubris and preening was always a component of the psychology of hip-hop, we see the Bad Boy stable, Mase, Puff Daddy and Biggie Smalls in particular, making direct reference to designer clothing labels. Champagne, luxury homes, luxury automobiles, and other markers of success, now become a routine part of the music. Hip-hop now has unprecedented access, resources and influence, tethered to its notoriety. Hip-hop is demonstrating greater self-awareness, mindfulness of expanding growing pains, and is becoming more reflective.

In this stage, we are given glimpses of hip-hop's development and rapid maturation. Hip-hop is taking more time to speak of the self and is branching creatively. In this developmental stage and space, we see Nas's release of "Illmatic" in 1994. While as brooding as "The Message" and as lyrical as Eric B. and Rakim's earliest works, "Illmatic" combines elements, and often feels like a poetic, scholarly work. It is definitively an urban rap album, but the art has been elevated in its crafting. The Notorious BIG (Biggie Smalls) released "Ready to Die" in the same year, and with it, brought a more nuanced and varied awareness of hip-hop's self. "Ready to Die" presents a being fully immersed in their surroundings, noting means for survival in that setting, but also mindful of how they have been impacted by trauma. The work presents an unfiltered emotional self-report. Biggie Smalls speaks about feelings of anguish, hopelessness, suicidality, depression, and regret. The work highlights the stressful duality of urban life, unapologetically.

During this stage of development, Dr. Dre and Outkast release "The Chronic" (1992) and "Southernplayalisticadillacmuzik" (1994), respectively. Each work represented a finely honed and fully realized version of a voice from its region. Both works, from their beats, to their slang, speak to urban life on the West Coast and in the deep South. In what in this stage, during the Source Music Awards, where

Andre 3000 of Outkast proclaimed, in the middle of East/West tensions that, "the South got something to say!"

It was in this stage that hip-hop found a new voice and icons. The competing selves and narratives produced iconic figures in Big Pun, Biggie Smalls, and Tupac, but each died tragically during this period. Hip-Hop, for the first time in its development, was having to cope with major loss and grief.

The Idol Worship stage sees hip-hop become more tribal, more superficial, more boastful, increasingly confident, and more secure in its position in world culture. This emotional comfort is likely what activates the creative diversity which emerges in the stage. Hip-Hop is looking upon itself, beginning to be "worshipped" as an art and music form, occupying greater spaces, and growing.

STAGE 4: THE GREAT MIGRATION/INTERNALIZATION (2001–2008)

In this stage of identity development, Cross (1971, 1991) indicates that a being now becomes more secure in their identity having lived with it, and is now more willing and open to having meaningful relationships with others who respect and value their identity. With regard to Black racial identity, this would represent an individual with a strong Black racial identity opening themselves up to relationships with diverse others who acknowledge and value their sense of being Black.

In the early to mid-2000s, hip-hop has entered true maturity, middle adulthood, and is firmly established. With regard to its identity development, hip-hop is now everywhere, has migrated and lived, and is beginning to move on to assuming other senses of self. Where the first 3 stages were largely seen to incorporate the story and waves and shifts of large Eastern, Midwestern and Western urban centers, the mid-2000s ushered in, fully, the story of the South. With this move and transition, came an emotional lifestyle change for hip-hop. The wordsmith crafted a story around the beat. The sound, and psychology, of the South, expanded the scope of hip-hop. Southern homegrown and supported record labels such as Cash Money and No Limit Records began to influence the sound and feel of hip-hop. In the South, the wordsmith was expected to partner with the beat. Reports of what was happening in one's home were meant to be coupled with a kind of celebration. Artists like Lil Wayne, Ludacris, T.I. and others brought about a cultural shift in hip-hop's fashion, lingo, sound, and feel.

The identity shift was seismic. In the same space were the elder statesmen of Hip-Hop from the East and Midwest continuing to make music (Jay Z, Nas, Eminem), while the South was producing its own elders (Outkast, Scarface) and crafting a sound which would come to define hip-hop for a generation. Hip-hop, as a being, was developing active, diverse relationships with a variety of sounds and content. There was still gangsta rap to be found, alongside still "conscious" artists in the form of Common and the Roots, with this new emerging Southern "trap" music sound, combining equal parts street/drug rap and celebration. Hip-hop had a sound for all occasions, and was commercially thriving, as a result.

STAGE 5: COPING/COMMITMENT (2008–PRESENT)

In this stage, Cross (1971) first indicates that a being in this stage is now secure in their identity. The being has a distinct understanding of what their identity means to them. They have a personal, profound sense of Blackness. The being translates this identity into a plan of action to benefit other Black people and/or to demonstrate a commitment to their group. This understanding and approach are sustained over time, and comfort with their racial identity and that of all others around them is maintained. For hip-hop in this stage, we saw a being growing sonically, merging sounds and cultural influences and strengthening its bonds with all of its regions and communities across the globe.

In this stage, we find hip-hop continually expanding, into a digital age that has simplified access and creation. The creators of the music have changed, trended younger (21 Savage, Young Thug, Drake, Kendrick Lamar) and who/what is hip-hop has now shifted. Influence is no longer charted by record sales alone, but in social media reach, concert attendance, and mentions. Here is a being with a rapidly evolving identity, and a goal toward expansion, influence, and prosperity. Hip-hop has become a world cultural force, producing artists and sounds native to all of the spaces where hip-hop is engaged and shared.

In the United States, hip-hop now has several apparently disparate "selves." The strong, regional tribalism of the past generation is less apparent, as artists are able to collaborate using new digital platforms. The regional sound is now blurred, as the Southern sound begins to dominate. As in all past stages, an identity emerges with its own look, sound, and feel. While there are still younger artists producing very lyrical rap music, there is a part of hip-hop's self which emerges and is called "mumble rap."

Artists from the south (Migos, Young Thug, Travis Scott, Future) begin to craft a sound around their present environment and emotional focus. In this stage, hip-hop, as a being, is spending a part of its time discussing living, and having lived, a life of excess. Tales of selling drugs were a part of the identity of hip-hop in prior stages, often discussed as a means of survival and a result of generational poverty. In the commitment stage, where hip-hop is living with older and younger members of its diverse fan base and community, taking drugs becomes a part of the identity.

In prior stages, hip-hop's sound was crafted around its reality. Violence and bravado were weaved into much of the music, as that was a part of the developmental fabric of hip-hop's existence. So too had drug use become a significant part of hip-hop's present and growing developmental fabric. Where the prior violence gave rise to "gangsta" rap, the present reality gave birth to intoxicated, drug-fueled, "mumble" rap. The mixture of technology, access, youth, and drug use has ushered in a unique sound and arrives in an instant where hip-hop is as palatable to as many appetites as it has ever been.

In assessing hip-hop's development to this point, we see a being that is further pushing its sonic and developmental boundaries. It has lived with generational trauma, had to adjust to the demands of exposure to the wider society, matured in its voice and presentation, and becoming a more complex and versatile being.

While the being of hip-hop might appear somewhat scattered and consistent considering its many selves, the presentation of this being at present is consistent with all beings when considering identity development. That is, hip-hop is evolving, and not fixed in any one stage. It is demonstrating the fluidity of identity that most developing beings do (Helms, 1990).

SELF-ACTUALIZATION

Erikson, in his stages of development, suggested that individuals come to a point, in late adulthood, just prior to reaching our geriatric years, where we assess what, and who, we have nurtured. He named this stage generativity versus stagnation and indicated that we wish to nurture things that will outlast us, while in this stage (Harris, 2000). I would suggest that we see hip-hop now broadening its impact and influence, with its community using its presence and energy to expand the scope, identity, and culture of hip-hop.

Like most identity development models, Erikson's late adulthood/geriatric stages describe the psychology of an individual which is now focused on examining whether they have become self-actualized. He would go on to describe a process of "identity confusion" for beings who had not resolved all conflicts and crises prior to reaching late adulthood (Erikson, 1971). While used in a number of ways in Psychology and Social Science studies, the concept of self-actualization represents a realization, or fulfilling, of one's life, talent and developmental potential.

Self-actualization is a growing and evolving process, not necessarily a developmental plateau. Maslow described self-actualization as a psychological concept which emerges after all other survival (food, shelter) and emotional (connection, intimacy) needs are met (Thalberg, 1964). Once the being has satisfied all prior needs, they can psychologically begin to explore who they have been and wish to be. The being may begin to explore the kinds of relationships they wish to maintain and develop, creative and personal pursuits which interest them, and ways in which they can satisfy the questions related to "who am I?"

Both Maslow and Rogers (1952) noted that self-actualization required autonomy and agency if one were to explore the concept successfully. Throughout its identity development, hip-hop has been faced with the same challenges to personal agency and self-direction as having the Black and Brown communities which embody and influence hip-hop culture. Erikson (1966) described the difficulty in African Americans developing a full and realized identity as the African American is "alienated from the world in which he is born and from the country of which he is a citizen" (p. 145). Hip-hop has had to manage crises of survival, safety, and development of core values, prior to being able to explore what it would mean to self-actualized.

Now, after growing through stages where hip-hop has maintained itself, established its voice and space, given birth to generations of artists and grown as an art form, it has now begun branching out with its voice and influence. Hip-hop has developed toward space where it is engaging the social, health and political challenges which face its communities. While still growing in influence and remaining a cultural and musical force, hip-hop is finding its civic voice. Considering its earliest stages, hip-hop has made self-actualization a goal, and in this stage, is working toward that goal.

At present, hip-hop is being studied as a science, and its content being leveraged toward improving urban classroom and college education (Kelly, 2013; Petchauer, 2011), as a sociopolitical force (Cooper, 2013) and for exploring issues of gender, power, and sexuality in urban communities (Dunbar, 2013). Hip-Hop is being introduced as an instrument, in many contexts, capable of healing, healing others, and promoting healthy development (Smith, 2019). Hip-Hop, as a being, has emerged as a core instrument of cultural change in a number of movements (HipHopEd, HipHopCivics) designed to promote access and equality.

Artists like Blue Scholars, Vince Staples and Chance The Rapper are broadening the self-reflective and political scope of hip-hop music to incorporate a voice focused on how youthful hip-hop is experiencing its world sociopolitically. Bruce Franks, known in the Battle rap community as Oops, has carried his civil rights/community focused message over into his role as a Missouri State Congressman. Rapsody, Boog Brown, Jean Grae, and Lady Leshurr are expanding the ways in which we experience women in hip-hop, presenting assertive and fully formed voices, sounds and identities.

While conversations around mental health and wellness have historically been taboo in the communities that contribute to hip-hop (Collins, Wong, Cerully, & Roth, 2014; Masuda, Anderson, & Edmonds, 2012) more and more artists have developed the voice and identity empowered to engage publicly in the discourse regarding their own struggles, and those they see in their communities and families

(Hinton, 2017). Styles P., DMX, Kid Cudi, Isaiah Rashad, Big Krit, Scarface, Joe Budden, and others have discussed their various symptoms and how these have impacted their lives and music.

Additionally, Young M.A., Syd, and Zebra Katz are expanding the conversation around sexuality in hip-hop, steering the community away from its long-held history of homophobia and transphobia. We are in a space with hip-hop where it is evolving quickly and demonstrating greater personal growth and diversity.

Beginning with four cultural "elements" (rapping, djing, breakdancing, graffiti art), hip-hop has grown to incorporate as many as ten unique elements if one considers rapping, break dancing, djing/beat making, beatboxing, fashion, language/patois, education, ownership/community building, health/wellness and advocacy/activism.

These are consistent with a developed being, and considering the always growing and new base of artists who engage hip-hop, suggest that the identity will remain an evolving one.

REFERENCES

Aidi, H. (2011). The grand (hip-hop) chessboard: Race, rap and raison d'État. *Middle East Report*, *260*, 25–39.

Alridge, D. (2005). From civil rights to hip hop: Toward a nexus of ideas. *The Journal of African American History*, *90*(3), 226–252.

Barnett, M., & Flynn, J. (2014). A century of celebration: Disrupting stereotypes and portrayals of African Americans in the media. *Black History Bulletin*, *77*(2), 28–33.

Bender, S. (2003). Eradicating Stereotypes: Community-Based Strategies of Media Counterspeech and Protest. In *Greasers and gringos: Latinos, law, and the American imagination* (pp. 169–186). New York, NY/London, England: NYU Press.

Bilodeau, B. and Renn, K. (2005). Analysis of LGBT identity development models and implications for practice. *Gender Identity and Sexual Orientation: Research, Policy and Personal*, *111*, 29–39.

Collins, R., Wong, E., Cerully, J., & Roth, E. (2014). *Racial and ethnic differences in mental illness stigma in California* (pp. 1–4). Santa Monica, CA: RAND Corporation.

Cooper, B. (2013). "Maybe I'll be a poet, rapper": Hip-hop feminism and literary aesthetics in "push". *African American Review*, *46*(1), 55–69.

Cornyetz, N. (1994). Fetishized blackness: Hip hop and racial desire in contemporary Japan. *Social Text*, (41), 113–139.

Cross, W.E., Jr. (1991). *Shades of black: Diversity in African-American identity*. Philadelphia, PA: Temple University Press.

Cross, W.E., Jr. (1971). The Negro-to-Black conversion experience: Toward a psychology of Black liberation. *Black World*, *20*, 13–27.

Dunbar, E. (2013). Hip hop (feat. women writers): Reimagining black women and agency through hip hop fiction. In L. King & S. Moody-Turner (Eds.), *Contemporary African American literature: The living canon* (pp. 91–112). Bloomington: Indiana University Press.

Erikson, E. (1966). The concept of identity in race relations: Notes and queries. *Daedalus*, *95*(1), 145–171.

Erikson, E. (1971). Notes on the life cycle. *Ekistics*, *32*(191), 260–265.

Gay, G. (1985). Implications of selected models of ethnic identity development for educators. *The Journal of Negro Education*, *54*(1), 43–55.

Hamilton, J. (2011). Pieces of a man. *Transition*, *106*, 113–126.

Harris, B. (2000). Review of the book *Identity's Architect: A Biography of Erik H. Erikson*. *The Journal of Interdisciplinary History*, *30*(4), 659–660.

Helms, J. E. (Ed.). (1990). Contributions in Afro-American and African studies, No. 129. In *Black and white racial identity: Theory, research, and practice*. New York, NY: Greenwood Press.

Hill, M.L. (2009). *Beats, rhymes, and classroom life: Hip-hop pedagogy and the politics of identity*. New York, NY: Teachers College Press.

Hinton, A. (2017). 'And so I bust back': Violence, race, and disability in hip hop. *CLA Journal*, *60*(3), 290–304.

Hughes, M., Kiecolt, K. J., Keith, V. M., & Demo, D. H. (2015). Racial identity and well-being among African Americans. *Social Psychology Quarterly*, *78*(1), 25–48.

Kelly, L. (2013). Hip-hop literature: The politics, poetics, and power of hip-hop in the english classroom. *The English Journal*, *102*(5), 51–56.

Lehman, Paul C. (2006). Civil rights in twilight: The end of the civil rights movement era in 1973. *Journal of Black Studies*, *36*(3), 415–428.

Lott, T. (1991). A no-theory theory of contemporary black cinema. *Black American Literature Forum*, *25*(2), 221–236.

Mahon, M. (2000). Black like this: Race, generation, and rock in the post-civil rights era. *American Ethnologist*, *27*(2), 283–311.

Masuda, A., Anderson, P., & Edmonds, J. (2012). Help-seeking attitudes, mental health stigma, and self-concealment among African American college students. *Journal of Black Studies*, *43*(7), 773–786.

McDermott, M., & Samson, F. (2005). White racial and ethnic identity in the United States. *Annual Review of Sociology*, *31*, 245–261.

Morant, K. (2011). Language in action: Funk music as the critical voice of a post—civil rights movement counterculture. *Journal of Black Studies*, *42*(1), 71–82.

Morgan, M., & Bennett, D. (2011). Hip-hop & the global imprint of a black cultural form. *Daedalus*, *140*(2), 176–196.

Papish, L. (2015). Promoting black (social) identity. *Social Theory and Practice*, *41*(1), 1–25.

Petchauer, E. (2011). Knowing what's up and learning what you're not supposed to: Hip-hop collegians, higher education, and the limits of critical consciousness. *Journal of Black Studies*, *42*(5), 768–790.

Quinn, E. (2010). "Tryin' to get over": "super fly", black politics, and post—civil rights film enterprise. *Cinema Journal*, *49*(2), 86–105.

Rogers, C. (1952). A personal formulation of client-centered therapy. *Marriage and Family Living*, *14*(4), 341–361.

Scott, M. (2005). The revolution will not be televised: Exploring contemporary social justice issues in the united states. *Black History Bulletin*, *68*(1), 24–29.

Smith, E. (2019). Discussing suicide without being crucified: The new renaissance of mental health in hip-hop. In Ransaw T., Gause C., & Majors R. (Eds.), *The handbook of research on black males: Quantitative, qualitative, and multidisciplinary* (pp. 591–610). East Lansing: Michigan State University Press.

Thalberg, I. (1964). A. H. Maslow's "Toward a Psychology of Being" [Book Review]. *Philosophy and Phenomenological Research, 25*(2), 288.

Yip, T., Sellers, R., & Seaton, E. (2006). African American racial identity across the lifespan: Identity status, identity content, and depressive symptoms. *Child Development, 77*(5), 1504–1517.

CHAPTER FIVE

The Miseducation of Urban Youth

Knowledge of Self in Therapy as Liberation from Racial Trauma

MARIEL BUQUE

@marielbuque

My emancipation don't fit your equation.

—Lauryn Hill

THE POSSIBILITY OF FREEDOM

I am free. Emancipated. And I am an AfroLatina. Emphasis on the [Afro]. You see, the way you present yourself to the world says a lot about who you are and where your priorities lie. And mine lies in the saliency of my Black identity and the whole premise of what it means to be Black and free within the context of mental health. Because Black Minds Matter. But I didn't start there.

I started this journey where my identities and educational roots took their form, in my beloved hometown of Newark, New Jersey, which is adjacent to Lauryn Hill's home of East Orange, which she lovingly calls out in her album *The Miseducation of Lauryn Hill*. For as long as I can remember, *Brick City* AKA *Da Bricks*, as we lovingly call the city of Newark, New Jersey, has always burgeoned with urban talent and creativity. But, how much of that talent goes untapped and unacknowledged? I don't have a census for that, but it's safe to say that a fair amount of the urban youth within our city has a lot to give this world and little chance to materialize those gifts because we start our journey through life being miseducated about who we are. In her album, Lauryn Hill uses her lyrics to take us back to her past while engaging in self-reflection and exemplifying the fifth element of hip-hop, knowledge of self, which aims at expanding urban youth's knowledge of themselves and their community to bring about action against inequities

(Akom, 2009; Love, 2018; Rose, 2018). In my work, I aim to work with urban youth to help them embody their knowledge of self. I couple the rich resources found in the fifth element of hip-hop with the emotional tools that help hip-hop youth navigate the emotional labor of self-learning with greater ease and a lessened vulnerability to racial trauma. That is the framework for my therapeutic work and the groundwork for the words that follow.

I remember my days as a youngin' in Newark as a moment of abundant resilience, but also as a time where our community needed to be affirmed and loved in the face of constant violence and adversity. Looking back to these days, I wonder just how many of us made our circumstances work in the face of so much dearth. Then I realized, this isn't the first time we've gone through extreme deficits, and that the emancipation I seek for our people doesn't lie in the power of oppressive structures. We carry the ancestral lessons and strength of those that came before us to make it through environments that are under-resourced and under-loved. As Mrs. Hill states in her song, *Lost Ones*, "wisdom is better than silver and gold." There is a lesson in our ancestral wisdom, and that knowledge is far too often omitted from our growth journey. Her work is liberatory artistry. It is intentionally emancipatory, in that it seeks to pour consciousness into our communities in an effort to help us liberate our minds from an oppressed mentality. It is the embodiment of the fifth element of hip-hop; self-knowledge. Similarly, Critical Hip Hop Pedagogy (CHHP) situates itself as a framework that disrupts oppressive structures and the damaging perceptions of urban youth that maintain the status quo (Akom, 2009). I place my therapeutic work within that same category. It is emancipatory, it is creative, it disrupts, and it is sacred art. To illustrate just how I frame therapy within a liberatory context, as Mrs. Hill did within her own work, as CHHP does within systems of education and mental health, I take to liberatory psychology to tap into how we can utilize ancestral knowledge to educate urban youth about their mental wellness and self-worth, before society steps in and miseducates them; before it steps in and miseducates (us).

MISEDUCATION BY OMISSION

Trauma is the person's reaction to an extreme injury. It can come from having something done to us, just as much as it can come from places of omission. As an educator or a therapist, if you omit truth and love from your work with a child, then the lesson you intended can easily disintegrate and the child can be left in a place of trauma. In her seminal book, *Why Are all the Black Kids Sitting Together in the Cafeteria?*, Dr. Beverly Daniel Tatum (2018) states that the historical information we receive about people of color, particularly that which is learned by omission, leaves behind negative assumptions that children carry about themselves, sometimes for life. Helping a child grow academically and emotionally without providing them with a pedagogy filled with the truth about their humanity is like planting a tree without tending to its roots. A rootless tree has no grounding, no solid footing, and these are common characteristics that we tend to see in children who struggle to hold themselves together in the face of racial adversity.

So where do we start to plant these roots? Well according to psychologist Randa Price (2010), two of the most influential environments that shape the minds of urban youth are the family and the school. These environments are the first points of intervention to help mediate the effects of the injustices they will face from all social institutions (Price, 2010). Synonymous to the use of hip hop as a liberatory practice within the framework of CHHP, therapy too can be rooted within the history of Black freedom struggle and the search for self-determination of marginalized communities (Akom, 2009; Martín-Baró, 1994).

I work as a psychology intern in both a hospital setting and within a high school close to where I grew up. There, I engage urban youth in monthly discussions about their communities, their identities, and how to sustain wellness as they develop their core sense of self. Within this self, lies many layers; one's self-worth, one's self-concept, one's self-esteem, and one's sense of safety. These conversations are a what I identify as a form of preventative intervention, that is to say, that they get ahead of the negative assumptions Dr. Tatum notes, and they get ahead of any mental health issue before it even has an opportunity to take root. It is one which gets ahead of the identity crises they will likely face, it gets ahead of the depression that can manifest in their lives, it gets in the way of impostor syndrome and any anxiety about doing well in school. It disrupts all of these possible mental health challenges by equipping them with the knowledge and tools they need in order to experience a sense of safety within a turbulent society and teaches them ways they can thrive in a world that was not built for their survival.

We generally go about life just developing into ourselves; the process of becoming. But how often do you hear about youth being taken out of their core curriculum to learn about something that's more pertinent and longer lasting than the content they gain from a lesson plan? During the monthly discussions that I hold within the high school, where I also provide therapy and workshops about mental health, the identity formation and emotional experiences of urban youth are centralized. That part of their edification is no longer excluded from the equation. Instead, they come to understand how to look at themselves and the urban landscape they call home in a positive light. This disrupts Mrs. Lauryn Hill's concept of miseducation and instills in urban youth a positive self-identity that is filled with truth and knowledge of self. As such, these conversations are a form of using self-knowledge as a form of freedom. The more Hip-hop youth know about their emotions and how they are tied to their identities, the more empowered they can become as they develop a core sense of themselves. During these conversations, we work on tangible skills to reframe their inner voice and ensure that it's working to continuously uplift them because much of the work we have to do to stay well comes from within. According to racial identity researcher and psychologist William Cross (1978), a critical aspect of the self-worth for our youth is the founding of racial identity. Therefore, once children have a general sense of what one's is and that it is attached to a positive racial identity, we can, and must, begin to talk about, racism, positionality, and safety. We must talk about how inculcating hip-hop in our work with urban youth can vehicle facilitate self-emancipation, communal emancipation, social justice, and political organizing (Akom, 2009).

YOU IS BLACK

Despite popular belief, racial awareness is developed in the mind of a child very early in life. Pipes McAdoo, (2002) offers an understanding of how racial awareness develops in children and how it becomes one of the earlier parts of one's identity that crystallizes. According to McAdoo, a recognition in *racial differences* begins to develop around ages 2–3, depending on how much a child has been exposed to variable races or skin types (Pipes McAdoo, 2002). During the ages 3–4, *racial identification* with a specific group occurs. I like to call this the crayon age, because like my nephew, an urban Black boy himself, once did at this age, kids start naming people's skin color according to the colors represented in their crayon boxes. I remember my nephew calling lighter folx in our family "the peach crayon" while the darker folx were referred to as "the brown crayon." Positive and negative phenotype attributes develop around this age as well. In the well documented and seminal 1940s doll and skin color preference studies by psychologists Kenneth and Mammie Clark (1939, 1940, 1947), in which they asked school-aged children about their racial preferences of dolls, the Clarks placed Black and White dolls in front of children and asked them to identify positive (i.e., pretty, good) and negative (i.e., ugly, bad) attributes to these dolls. As proven in their original studies and many more replicated studies thereafter, the Black dolls would almost exclusively be assigned the negative attributes, while the white dolls retained all the good traits. If a child sees a Black doll that they identify with as "bad" or "ugly," it is safe to say that they are simultaneously internalizing those attributes toward themselves. This was illustrated in Clark and Clark's (1947) color preference studies in which children were also asked to draw themselves in the color that they would prefer to be and children continuously rejected the use of brown crayons to draw themselves, even when this color most closely matched their own skin color, indicating that these colors were undesirable.

CHHP helps us to understand this internalization of self-worth, through the messages that school systems create around neo indigenous youth, as Chris Emdin

(2016) refers to them in his book *For White Folks Who Teach in the Hood and the Rest of Y'all Too* He refers to the ways in which educators uproot local indigenous value and replace it with Western deals that leave urban youth emotionally and educationally disenfranchised (Emdin, 2016). The Clarks correlated this systemic disenfranchisement to the racist messages that youth internalize and, correlated these internalized messages with wounded self-esteem (Clark & Clark, 1947). When that racial group membership doesn't become salient or when a preference for whiteness internalizes, as was the case with it would with the children in the Clark studies, it would inevitably lead to negative beliefs about oneself and about one's racial community, and ultimately result in mental distress (Fulmore, Taylor, Ham, & Lyles, 1994; Guthrie, 1976; Pipes McAdoo, 2002). At the completion of these studies, now more than 70 years ago, the Clarks called for the construction of mental hygiene programs that would relieve a child of color from the "tremendous burden of feelings of inadequacy and inferiority, which seem to become integrated into the very structure of the personality they develop" (Clark & Clark, 1947, p. 350).

How come we ain't getting no higher?

—Lauryn Hill

THE PERVASIVENESS OF RACIAL TRAUMA

Helping children develop into well-functioning adults who can survive and thrive within a racist society is no easy feat. It takes a village. On all ends, we must affirm the humanity of urban youth, before that humanity suffers multiple racial injuries. For urban youth in educational systems, these racial injuries take the form of alienation from traditional school environments and omission from learning that represents their own organic, self-expression (Alim & Pennycook, 2007; Emdin, 2010; Ladson-Billings, 2018; Rose, 2018). This hindrance in their freedom of expression is a racial injury that extends for many years of being in a miseducating system of instruction. The noted effects of racism have been identified as including both physical health problems and psychological disturbances (Comas-Diaz, 2016; Ong, Fullerr, Rowell, & Burrow, 2009). Most notably, has been the pervasive sense that the racial injury is out of one's control and will soon happen again. This hypervigilance is one of the key markers of trauma. And because racist attacks occur with frequency in institutions built on racist ideologies, the targets of racism are often accurate in their fear of an incoming attack and often experience retraumatization when the subsequent attack actually happens (Bryant-Davis & Ocampo, 2006; Comas-Díaz, 2007).

Many times, within communities in which trauma is an intergenerational phenomenon, racial trauma doesn't just begin with exposure to oppressive environments but is instead carried in one's lineage. In the womb, a traumatized mother is capable of genetically transmitting specific biomarkers that produce pathophysiological alterations in the baby's newborn body; leaving a child susceptible to genetic risk factors, that when matched with oppressive environments, can predispose the baby to traumatic reactions. To explain this more concretely, the trauma that a mother experiences, alters her genetically. Those genetic markers, which carry within them these traumas, have demonstrated to possess neurobiological abnormalities in patients with traumatic stress, which pose a biological vulnerability for future generations to become susceptible to traumatic stress (Sherin & Nemeroff, 2011; van der Kolk, 2014). And so these genes make the child biologically vulnerable when confronted with a traumatic event like racism (Sherin & Nemeroff, 2011). Trauma then becomes intergenerational (Dunbar & Blanco, 2013; Comas-Diaz 2016; van der Kolk, 2005). A history of racial oppression, in addition to contemporary racial injuries, can result in the development of traumatic reactions among folx of color (Bryant-Davis & Ocampo, 2006; Dunbar & Blanco, 2013). That is why every time I see a person of color enter my office, I see them with immense compassion. I know that somewhere in their lineage, there was trauma. With almost precise certainty, I can connect at least one of their psychological conditions back to the effects of oppressive structures. For hip-hop youth, racism can impose long-term psychological injuries before they are even able to fully understand the social consequences of racism. n this tech-driven age, children have been confronted with the murders of their peers, Trayvon Martin, Tamir Rice, Cameron Tillman, VonDerrit Myers Jr., Laquan McDonald, countless others and aren't preemptively equipped to actively process these deaths. I cringe at the sound of another Black child's name is listed among those murdered. I still feel intense emotions upon seeing Trayvon's pictures. "He was a little boy," I say to myself, almost to find a way to explicate his innocence, but it just fuels the hurt. So if that is me, an adult with 7 years of psychology training under her belt, what could possibly be going on in the minds of Black children when they see this image? The answer, silent chaos.

In the podcast, Black Boys & Men: Changing the Narrative, host Jayson K. Jones, alongside, the Director of the McSilver Institute for Poverty Policy and Research at the NYU Silver School of Social Work Dr. Michael Lindsey, Ph.D., MSW, MPH create a picture of the suicide epidemic among Black children. As it currently stands, the suicide rate of Black children within the ages of 5–11 has doubled over this past generation. Black boys and Latina girls are those most affected, resulting in this nation's largest population of suicides. So to answer Mrs. Hill's question *"How* come we ain't getting no higher?"* It's because our pain runs deep, through the generations.

RACIAL TRAUMA IN THE SCHOOLS

Discrimination is not always experienced as concrete situations that we can point out (Ferguson-Peters, 2002). When it's embedded in the undercurrent of the school operations, it can be harder to detect. What is, however, more visible is the externalized behaviors of urban youth, which often signal that something is up. Many times, these externalized behaviors are the representations of the suffering that has been endured by that student, which is usually marked by fear, anger, and depression. If we decide to only see the surface level issue which is represented as externalized behaviors (i.e., oppositional defiance, attention deficit hyperactivity disorder, etc.), we miss the bigger picture of what's truly happening, which is that a child might suffering, in silence. I've heard numerous clients relay how they've felt disturbed by their teachers' remarks and misunderstood by administrators when attempting to secure their emotional safety. These are the kids we see are villain-ized by the school system which proceeds to punish the student and leave the teacher free of any consequence to their racial assault. That is racial trauma.

I often refer back to my earlier years and wonder why more people didn't spend the exuberant amount of free time we had, to elevate our minds. I remember needing more from my teachers, but receiving only a portion of what I needed, and therefore feeling disconnected from my own learning process. Since I identify as a former Hip-hop youth myself, whose knowledge of herself, her peers and her community at large stemmed from the art and culture reflected in Hip-hop, I am now finding myself at a point of reflection about how much some of my own teachers missed the mark on applying a pedagogical approaches the rich culture found in Hip-hop. I reflect on this more as an adult, due to the exposure I've had to CHHP through interactions with my friends and colleagues and hip-hop ped-agogies Courtney Rose and Edmund Adjapong, through the weekly #HipHopEd twitter chats that inside so much energy through social media, and through the lectures by Yolanda Sealey-Ruiz, Chris Emdin, and Bettina Love that I've been blessed to hear. My exposure to the freedom of expression that is emphasized in CHHP brought me to an understanding of my own miseducation, the ways that the self-knowledge I could have been grounded on was stolen from me, and the ways in which I constantly work to unlearn the parts of my identity that came from what Freire coined as the banking system of education (Freire, 1972). My interac-tions with these scholars and their work have helped me understand that although I can't go back and eradicate the unfortunate ways that I had been un-taught, and I can't undo the collective trauma that has poured out of schools and into our children's minds, that I can do the work now. I can work on reconciling the anger I held onto for being miseducated and the trauma of holding on to an inauthentic version of myself for so long. I can be free of all of that pain and I can pay that lesson forward. We are living in generations of trauma that are marked by the injustices we face. So I choose to frame my psychology-based work around getting us to higher ground and through the liberation of these traumas. I look to convert the injustices represented in our educational experiences into justice-oriented work with youth in schools and mental-health related work.

Hip-hop youth often come into my therapy office spaces feeling hurt; emotionally wounded by the transgressions of their schools. "They only see how I react," they say when they're being held in the principal's office for externalizing their pain in unproductive behaviors. They rightfully feel rage and sadness when they feel chronically misunderstood by teachers and society at large. They are so frequently deprived of some of the most basic human needs on every level of the human hierarchy of needs because the classroom operates as a breeding ground for traumatic experiences (Atkins & Harmon, 2016; Emdin, 2016). Their sense of safety is compromised within school structures that oppress them, their psychological needs of love and a sense of belonging are lacking in schools where students are unseen by teachers. Their ability to maintain healthy self-esteem that relies on elders' view of them is inhibited, and their capacity to feel a sense of accomplishment that matches their full potential is thwarted when their efforts are met with disapproval. According to Emdin (2016), teachers contribute to the collective impact of the psyche of urban youth. So when students' basic human expression is being disregarded, how then could we expect them to engage in active and productive learning while in school? If they are constant targets of racial injustice, rather than the targets of love and nurturance, how can we expect them to thrive in educational systems? Racial bias towards urban youth has historically topped the detention/suspension/expulsion charts and has been an important marker in generating the school-to-prison pipeline. This process of villainizing and misunderstanding urban youth that must be dismantled. And because the environment is at the core of the issue, the environment, including teachers and administrators, must be at the center of the solution. It is the responsibility of educators to operate as a vehicle for the positive identity development of urban youth. If one chooses to work with urban youth, one must be held accountable for nurturing their racial-ethnic development and infusing them with love, an emotion that is key for basic survival.

How you gon' win when you ain't right within?

—Lauryn Hill

SELF-KNOWLEDGE AS AN EMANCIPATORY THERAPEUTIC PRACTICE

The fifth element of hip-hop, knowledge of self, offers an avenue for enhancing the critical consciousness and collective consciousness of students (Adjapong, 2017).

Given that Mrs. Hill's album operates as a motivator for my work with youth, I ask myself how I can embody Lauryn Hill's quest for people to feel inspired and uplifted by their community. In her song *Superstar*, she urges artists to "light [her] fire" by taking Hip-hop back to its root purpose of centering the narratives of communities of color within a sociopolitical act of resistance and freedom of expression. More than twenty years after the drop of her album, I want to take on that challenge by helping to infuse that fire in hip-hop youth in therapy spaces, to push them to help them hold a mirror to society as Akom (2009) intended for the work that embodies CHHP. I seek to help them unpack the problems they face and utilize transformational resistance that can uplift their minds, bodies, and souls, and do the same within their communities. And motivate them to embody an uplifted mind, body, soul and transmit that uplifted consciousness into their communities.

FREEDOM WORK: SELF-KNOWLEDGE AND THE DEVELOPMENT OF HEALTHY MINDS

In my approach toward developing healthy minds of urban youth, I take to Akom's work on Critical Hip Hop Pedagogy (2009), Martin Baro's (1994) liberatory psychology, Lillian Comas-Diaz's work on racial trauma recovery (Comas-Diaz, 2016), and Freire's conscientization (Freire, 1972), to develop a framework for the practice of liberating our people from mentalized oppression.

There are certain requisites to us getting free within the context of therapy. First therapy must be accessible to all. I developed a mental health directory that is for people of color, by people of color, *@CulturalTherapy* in order to attempt to bridge the gap that exists between people of color seeking mental health services and the practitioners who have been trained in culturally-informed mental health care and are committed to servicing racially minoritized communities. Beyond that, clinicians and clients alike, need to work together to assess the impact of racial trauma upon the client's life. Some of this information may be evident during the initial contact with a student, while some will surface in subsequent contact with that student over time, as both clinician and client may not be aware of the enormous influence of racism on the client's life. Remember trauma is embedded in our minds and bodies. The work to eradicate trauma is hard and long, but worthwhile.

DESTIGMATIZING MENTAL HEALTH

Because of the enormous stigma that is associated with mental illness and negative stereotypes around words like anxiety and depression, it is important that the activities that are introduced to urban youth, are presented with this in mind. I choose to present my activities to my students in ways that feel least pathologizing and pejorative and invite them to contribute to renaming their therapy-based activities in ways that help ease their discomfort. One such example is that of a group of teenage Black and Brown adolescent boys who I once counseled. Prior to my inheriting the group, it was called the *Attention Deficit Hyperactivity Disorder* group. As the first activity toward self-knowledge and self-empowerment, we collectively changed the name of the group and talked about the reasons why we changed it, the ways in which the previous name reinforces stereotypes about urban boys. The pejorative quality of the group name was in the name itself "deficit" and so, the first collective task we engaged in was taking the negative association out of the group's name. This is an important aspect of mental health work with urban youth, due to the pervasive racial health disparities that exist due to the stigma communities of color have towards mental health (Emdin, Adjapong, & Levy, 2016; Holm-Hansen, 2006).

As in Freire's (1972) work and in CHHP practice, I take on the role of facilitator of the group's ideas and change-oriented action. Together, the group members took action and later reflected on how we would transform the perceptions held of this group. Similarly, schools that have structures in place that seek to "remediate" students and embody pejorative names and approaches can be transformed into places of productive action for these students, in a way that humanizes them. Actively engaging students in this process always promote empowerment and self-efficacy in them that they would otherwise not get in other spaces. As they engage in practices that offer them freedom of expression, particularly as it relates to their mental wellness, they will themselves guide their own emancipation.

HIP-HOP MEDITATION AND MOVEMENT THERAPY

In my work and personal life, I live by the motto that we must *Heal as we Rise*, because I believe that our emancipatory process and our collective progress is dependent upon our collective wellness. Mrs. Hill's song *Doo Wop* raises the question of how we find our way into the straight path, with references on spiritual fasting "Sirat al-Mustaqim" and meditation in an effort to have a clear mind that welcomes acceptance into the new things we are able to learn. For urban youth, racial-cultural pride, resilience around the injustices they face, and spirituality are, to some degree, interwoven (Mattis & Mattis, 2011). Multiple scholars have interwoven aspects of spirituality and religion into their work with youth, through an understanding of its operative roots in healing. Take for example how Chris Emdin has infused reality pedagogy and the call-and-response technique into his work with urban youth, which has its roots in the Church, as he understood this to be a mechanism to keeping youth engaged in the work (Emdin, 2016). Mrs. Hill herself infuses her album with stories about how she embodied a spiritual quest in an effort to counter the miseducated state that she found herself in. Similarly, therapeutic techniques that derive from spirituality are operative in the quest towards meaning and healing in the mental health of urban people. It is understood, that people who derive from collectivistic cultures require therapeutic methods that value holism, like for example meditation and imagery which both guide the imagination to help the mind and body relax (Comas-Diaz, 2007). As such, I start my sessions at the intersection of holistic methods (meditation) and CHHP practice Hip-hop, to engage urban youth in a practice of *Hip hop-based meditation*. Together, we enter a state of peaceful consciousness with a Hip-hop instrumental playing in the back as the soundboard for healing. We use music's healing properties as a restorative practice. We also use these pieces of music to elicit movement in the therapy room where each person uses the rhythm of the music to shake off the stress that they bring through the door. Educators can similarly infuse this practice into the start of their class. A few minutes of engaging in hip-hop-infused meditative techniques can help students feel grounded for the lesson ahead and open their minds to engage much deeper in the learning experience.

CHANGING THE NARRATIVE THROUGH THERAPY

The narratives of urban youth are often constructed for them in ways that exclude their participation and thereby disallows them from creating self-narratives that truly reflect who they are. In narrative-based therapies, which invite Hip-hop youth to engage in the re-writing of their narratives with prompting questions, we engage in what Comas-Diaz (2016) calls wisdom enhancing, where we call upon ancestral wisdom to reframe internalized racist ideologies and change our own narratives. I would then engage the person in a follow-up conversation on their narrative, which I use as an act of psychological decolonization. The effort is to collectively enhance the resilience narrative, enhance cultural-racial pride, and debunk myths of dysfunction and deficit. It is a dialectical activity in which I borrow from the CHHP practice, where pedagogues create an emancipatory space, in which both student and educator are liberated (Rose, 2018). Together, we dismantle every aspect of our miseducation and we collectively taste freedom, because freedom is meant to liberate us all

Whether the work takes place in a school or a therapeutic setting, the main dynamic to consider is that we work "together" with urban youth to engage in on the liberation of the mind. We emancipate together. The work is centered on freeing students/clients from the intergenerational trauma, stereotypes, internalized oppression, and disconnection from their racial group by helping them take an active role in that liberatory journey.

When I was young, hip-hop deposited onto, me a larger understanding of who I was. As an adult, it continues to frame my identity and my liberation. Like Lauryn Hill, I suffered from miseducation that was offered by institutions of education. Somewhere in my journey, as did Lauryn, I underwent both the pain and triumph of self-discovery. And like most hip hop pedagogies, I realized in my academic journey that we must go back to hip hop as a point of discovery and liberation. And so, I intend on infusing knowledge of self into my daily work with urban youth, because I know, personally and professionally, that our roots hold the key to our emancipation. Here is where our work can be truly transformative.

I want to thank our living ancestor, Lauryn Hill for the wisdom and inspiration to produce this piece.

May you stay woke. May you stay well. And remember that we must *heal as we rise*.

In Decolonization, Asè.

REFERENCES

Adjapong, E. S. (2017). Bridging theory and practice in the urban science classroom: A framework for hip-hop pedagogy in STEM. *Critical Education*, 8(15).

Akom, A. A. (2009). Critical hip hop pedagogy as a form of liberatory praxis. *Equity & Excellence in Education*, 42(1), 52–66.

Samy Alim, H., & Pennycook, A. (2007). Glocal linguistic flows: Hip-hop culture (s), identities, and the politics of language education. *Journal of Language, Identity, and Education*, 6(2), 89–100.

Atkins, W.A., & Harmon, A. (2016). Maslow's hierarchy of needs. In Gale (Ed.), *Gale encyclopedia of children's health: Infancy through adolescence* (3rd ed.). Farmington, MI: Gale.

Martín-Baró, I., & Martín-Baró, I. (1994). *Writings for a liberation psychology.* Harvard University Press.

Bryant-Davis, T., & Ocampo, C. (2006). A therapeutic approach to the treatment of racist incident-based trauma. *Journal of Emotional Abuse*, 6, 1–22.

Clark, K., & Clark, M. (1939). The development of consciousness of self and the emergence of racial identity in Negro preschool children. *Journal of Social Psychology*, 10, 591–599.

Clark, K., & Clark, M. (1940). Skin color as a factor in racial identification of Negro preschool children. *Journal of Social Psychology*, 11, 159–169.

Clark, K., & Clark, M. (1947). Racial identification and preference in Negro children. In T. Newcomb & E. Hartley (Eds.), *Readings in social psychology* (pp. 602–611). New York, NY: Henry Holt.

Comas-Díaz, L. (2007). Ethnopolitical psychology: Healing and transformation. In E. Aldarondo (Ed.), *Promoting social justice in mental health practice* (pp. 91–118). Hillsdale, NJ: Erlbaum.

Comas-Díaz, L. (2016). Racial trauma recovery: A race-informed therapeutic approach to racial wounds. In A.N. Alvarez, C.T.H. Liang, & H.A. Neville (Eds.), *Cultural, racial, and ethnic psychology book series. The cost of racism for people of color: Contextualizing experiences of discrimination* (pp. 249–272). Washington, DC: American Psychological Association.

Cross, W.E., Jr. (1978). The Thomas and Cross models of psychological nigrescence: A review. *Journal of Black Psychology, 5,* 13–31.

Dunbar, E., & Blanco, A. (2013). Psychological perspectives on culture, violence, and intergroup animus: Evolving traditions in the bonds that tie and hate. In F.T.L. Leong (Ed.), *APA handbook of multicultural psychology* (pp. 378–399). Washington, DC: American Psychological Association.

Emdin, C. (2010). *Urban science education for the hip hop generation: Essential tools for the science educator and researcher.* Rotterdam, The Netherland: Sense Publishers.

Emdin, C. (2016). *For white folks who teach in the hood—and the rest of y'all too: Reality pedagogy and urban education,* Boston, MA: Beacon Press.

Emdin, C., Adjapong, E., & Levy, I. (2016). Hip-hop based interventions as pedagogy/therapy in STEM. *Journal for Multicultural Education, 10*(3), 307–321.

Ferguson-Peters, M. (2002). Racial socialization of young Black children. In H.P. McAdoo (Ed.), *Black children: Social, educational, and parental environments,* (pp. 57–72). Thousand Oaks, CA: Sage.

Freire, P. (1972). *Pedagogy of the oppressed.* New York, NY: Herder and Herder.

Fulmore, C., Taylor, T., Ham, D., & Lyles, B. (1994). Psychological consequences of internalized racism. *Psych Discourse, 24*(10), 12–15.

Guthrie, R.V. (1976). *Even the rat was white: A historical view of psychology.* New York, NY: Harper and Row.

Holm-Hansen, C. (2006), *Racial and ethnic disparities in children's mental health.* Saint Paul, MN: Wilder Research.

Ladson-Billings, G. (2018). The social funding of race: The role of schooling. Peabody *Journal of Education, 93*(1), 90–105.

Love, B.L. (2018). Knowledge reigns supreme: The fifth element of critical hip-hop pedagogy & community. In C. Emdin & E. Adjapong (Eds.), *#hipHopEd: The compilation on hip-hop education.* Rotterdam, The Netherland: Sense Publishers.

Martín-Baró, I. (1994). *Writings for a liberation psychology.* Cambridge, MA: Harvard University Press.

Mattis, J.S., & Mattis, J.H. (2011). Religiosity and spirituality in the lives of African American children. In N.E. Hill, T.L. Mann, & H.E. Fitzgerald (Eds.), *Child psychology and mental health. African American children and mental health, Vol. 1: Development and context, Vol. 2: Prevention and social policy.* Santa Barbara, CA: Praeger/ABC-CLIO.

McAdoo, P. (2002). *Black children: Social, educational, and parental environments.* New Delhi, India: Sage Publications.

Ong, A.D., Fuller-Rowell, T., & Burrow, A.L. (2009). Racial discrimination and the stress process. *Journal of Personality and Social Psychology, 96*(6), 1259–1271.

Price, R., (2010). *Psychology, race equality and working with children.* Stoke-on-Trent, England: Trentham Books.

Rose, C. (2018). Toward a critical hip hop pedagogy for teacher education. In C. Emdin & E. Adjapong (Eds.), *#hipHopEd: The compilation on hip-hop education.* Rotterdam, The Netherland: Sense Publishers.

Sherin, J.E., & Nemeroff, C.B. (2011). Post-traumatic stress disorder: The neurobiological impact of psychological trauma. *Dialogues in Clinical Neuroscience, 13*(3), 263–278.

Tatum, B.D. (2018) *"Why are all the black kids sitting together in the cafeteria?": And other conversations about race.* New York, NY: Basic Books.

van der Kolk, B. A. (2005). Attachment, self-regulation, and competency, a comprehensive intervention framework for children with complex trauma. Psychiatric Annals, 35(5), 424–430.

van der Kolk, B. A. (2014). *The body keeps the score: Brain, mind, and body in the healing of trauma.* New York, NY: Penguin Books.

PART II

Social and Emotional Learning through Hip Hop Education

CHAPTER SIX

When 16 Ain't Enough

Moving beyond Emotional Evocation

IAN LEVY

@IanPLevy

Discussions of mental health, or expressing social and emotional difficulties, have become more prevalent in hip hop lyrics over time. Historically, speaking about one's emotions over a beat, without highlighting one's perseverance, has been lambasted as "soft," "fake" or inauthentic in hip hop culture (McLeod, 1999). In 2009 however, Kid Cudi's dropped Soundtrack to My Life, marking a major shift in the emotional expressiveness of mainstream artists (Lafrance, Burns, & Woods, 2017). On this song (the single for the album), Kudi references emotions that he's kept hidden from the view of others, and the album went double platinum. This is interesting, given that in the 1990s LL Cool Jay's authenticity was publically challenged for pouring out his emotions. The response of hiding emotions in the face of adversity remains a gender normative approach rooted in the societal perception of emotions as a weakness (Randell, Jerdén, Öhman, Starrin, & Flacking, 2016). However, in contemporary times, billboard has boasted lyrics from rappers like the later Juice WRLD who spoke about sitting alone in a dark room while processing heartbreak. There appears to be more acceptance from the hip hop community regarding the evocation of emotion.

General research on emotions highlights that adolescents experience more emotional stress than any other age group, and are at an increased risk for developing a range of social and emotional problems (Guo, Nguyen, Weiss, Ngo, & Lau, 2015; Lin & Yusoff, 2013). An understanding of one's emotions, its causes, and consequences are essential to the well-being of all people (Wong & Rochlen, 2005). While the evocation of emotions is an important step in the navigation of emotional concerns, emotion-processing is required for healing to occur (Greenberg, 2004). Emotion-processing is the discussion and dissection of emotional experiences, to create mechanisms to cope, and ultimately to move past difficult events (Greenberg, 2004). The shift in willingness for the hip hop generation to speak about emotional experiences is laudable, but not enough. Amidst the increase in emotional expressiveness, access to quality mental health services is significantly less likely for Black and Latinx communities (Creedon & Lê Cook, 2016). Further, data shows two-thirds of adolescents have experienced a traumatic event prior to the age of 17, making them vulnerable to developing posttraumatic stress disorder (McLaughlin et al., 2013).

Levy, Emdin, and Adjapong (2018) explain that the hip-hop cypher has functioned as a cathartic outlet for the hip hop community to discuss thoughts and feelings, as a response to the lack of access to services. While hip hop community practices on their own have offered catharsis to the hip hop community, the purposeful inclusion of these practices in counseling sessions, as emotional-processing interventions, can help move beyond the mere evoking of emotions, towards deepening one's emotional self-awareness and ultimately healing (Levy, 2019). Chapters within this section of the volume present hip-hop based social and emotional programming for youth, geared towards supporting emotion-processing.

Gemma Connell opens this section by illuminating her experiences as a choreographer and dance facilitator based in the UK. Through personal use of hip hop dance and spoken word as a practitioner, Connell outlines a workshop curriculum which intends to support individuals in processing traumatic life experiences. As a teacher, Janine Brown bridges the gap between theory and practice with a first-hand account of her use of pedagogical approaches for social and emotional learning. Rooted in theory, and a personal narrative, Brown provides readers with a hands-on curriculum that they might use to support students' social and emotional growth in their classrooms. While a bevy of research points to the need to use hip-hop based counseling practices in urban schools (Elligan, 2004; Levy, 2019), seldom have scholars explored the applicability of hip hop based frameworks in career counseling. Drawing from their work in a career counseling center in California, Nate Nevado and Kim Davalos share an innovative approach to hip hop career counseling. This section closes with an evaluation of a hip hop and spoken word course at a High School in New York City. Beyond providing a replicable breakdown of a course designed to support students in navigating difficult thoughts and feelings, Qiana Spellman evidences the impact of this course on the lives of her students through the presentation of student lyrics and case studies. The authors in this section take the reader through the creation of curriculum, workshops, frameworks, and student lyrics which collectively support the use of hip hop based approaches for student's social and emotional growth.

REFERENCES

Creedon, T.B., & Lê Cook, B. (2016). Access to mental health care increased but not for substance use, while disparities remain. *Health Affairs; Chevy Chase, 35*(6), 1017–1021. http://dx.doi.org/10.1377/hlthaff.2016.0098

Elligan, D. (2004). Rap therapy: A practical guide for communicating with youth and young adults through rap music. Kensington Books.

Greenberg, L.S. (2004). Emotion-focused therapy. *Clinical Psychology & Psychotherapy: An International Journal of Theory & Practice, 11*(1), 3–16.

Guo, S., Nguyen, H., Weiss, B., Ngo, V.K., & Lau, A.S. (2015). Linkages between mental health need and help-seeking behavior among adolescents: Moderating role of ethnicity and cultural values. *Journal of Counseling Psychology, 62*(4), 682. doi: 10.1037/cou0000094

Lafrance, M., Burns, L., & Woods, A. (2017). Doing hip-hop masculinity differently: Exploring Kanye West's 808s & Heartbreak through word, sound, and image. In S. Hawkins, (Ed.), *The routledge research companion to popular music and gender* (pp. 303–317). Abingdon, UK: Routledge.

Levy, I. (2019). Hip-Hop and Spoken Word Therapy in Urban School Counseling. Professional School Counseling, 22(1b). DOI: 10.1177/2156759X19834436

Levy, I., Emdin, C., & Adjapong, E. S. (2018). Hip-Hop Cypher in Group Work. *Social Work with Groups, 41*(1–2), 103–110. https://doi.org/10.1080/01609513.2016.1275265

Lin, H. J., & Yusoff, M. S. B. (2013). Psychological distress, sources of stress and coping strategy in high school students. *International Medical Journal, 20*(6), 672–676.

McLaughlin, K.A., Koenen, K.C., Hill, E.D., Petukhova, M., Sampson, N.A., Zaslavsky, A.M., & Kessler, R.C. (2013). Trauma exposure and posttraumatic stress disorder in a national sample of adolescents. *Journal of the American Academy of Child & Adolescent Psychiatry*, 52(8), 815–830. doi: 10.1016/j.jaac.2013.05.011

McLeod, K. (1999). Authenticity within hip-hop and other cultures threatened with assimilation. *Journal of Communication, 49*(4), 134–150. https://doi.org/10.1111/j.1460-2466.1999.tb02821.x

Randell, E., Jerdén, L., Öhman, A., Starrin, B., & Flacking, R. (2016). Tough, sensitive and sincere: How adolescent boys manage masculinities and emotions. *International Journal of Adolescence and Youth, 21*(4), 486–498. https://doi.org/10.1080/02673843.2015.1106414

Wong, Y.J., & Rochlen, A.B. (2005). Demystifying men's emotional behavior: New directions and implications for counseling and research. *Psychology of Men & Masculinity, 6*(1), 62–72. https://doi.org/10.1037/1524-9220.6.1.62

CHAPTER SEVEN

Pass the Mic

The Therapeutic Potential of Hip Hop Education in Dance and Spoken Word

GEMMA CONNELL

@FutureHipHopDr

Tricia Rose (2008) once wrote "Hip hop is not dead, but it is gravely ill" (Rose, 2008, p. ix). Whilst I understand Rose's feelings in reference to the commercialisation of rap music and the loss of a feeling of community in some areas of Hip Hop, I cannot entirely agree with her. In my world, Hip Hop is saving lives. By that, I don't necessarily mean that it is performing heart surgery or curing cancer, but it is helping people who feel they have no way out of difficult life situations, to find a pathway through their struggles. Some of my evidence for this comes from my own experiences; I am a dancer and choreographer, and I truly believe that Hip Hop saved my life. I found Hip Hop dance at the age of ten. Since then, whenever I have experienced something difficult, Hip Hop has been there for me. After loss, heartbreak and depression, I threw myself into dance, which became my own form of personal therapy. Whilst I am aware that the term "therapy" is both a loaded and a protected term, I very much feel that Hip Hop has provided me with the opportunity to psychologically heal in many ways; whether that be using dance and spoken word to work through my own experiences of gender violence, or using dance as my escape in periods where I've lost loved ones.

I am a choreographer and dance facilitator based in the UK. This chapter forms a personal reflection on my artistic practice in facilitating workshops in Hip Hop dance and spoken word with specific community groups. I have delivered these workshops to women and children recovering from domestic violence and sexual abuse, stroke survivors and young adults with autism, down syndrome and Attention Deficit Hyperactivity Disorder (ADHD). These workshops were initially intended as a fun opportunity for the participants, but I have since discovered that the use of Hip Hop techniques provided participants with a sense of agency. By using these techniques, participants have been able to regain control over certain areas of their lives. For example, a stroke survivor, Sue*, felt that she would never be able to generate a piece of creative writing about her experiences of stroke, because she struggled to find the words to convey her emotions following her stroke. By creating a Hip Hop-inspired "remix" of an existing piece of spoken word, Sue was able to express herself through words. She was asked to rearrange the words, remove anything that she didn't agree with and change words or phrases to more accurately express her meaning. Sue didn't have to engage in the daunting task of writing spoken word from scratch; she remixed someone else's work, in order to express herself. It is this sense of agency that can help people move forward, and better deal with what they have been through.

I discovered my own sense of agency through Hip Hop when I choreographed my second solo dance theatre work in 2017. Entitled "Lies My Parents Told Me," this piece was initially inspired by generation gaps and how different generations now seem so ideologically far apart, that they don't understand each other anymore. Formed of Hip Hop dance and spoken word, this work very much dealt with relationships between mothers and daughters, and how the lessons that we pass down to our children aren't always positive. The creation of this work was a cathartic process. The use of Hip Hop techniques in dance and spoken word allowed me to begin to understand why my life had followed a certain path, what toxic behaviours I had inherited, and what I might do to change them. This experience, coupled with the variety of experiences I have facilitating Hip Hop dance and spoken word workshops in community settings, has led me to further research how the techniques that I use might be useful in therapeutic contexts.

THE POTENTIAL OF HIP HOP AND DANCE THERAPY

Globally, artists, psychologists and health practitioners are working to establish art therapies and creative methods for developing and sustaining a personal state of well-being (Bungay & Vella-Burrows, 2013). Some small studies have begun to establish that there is value in using creativity to "achieve positive change in the lives of people who have mental disorders" (Papagiamaki & Shinebourne, 2016) and in helping to combat the symptoms of postpartum depression and posttraumatic stress disorder, for example (Di Blasio et al., 2015). Practically, Hip Hop therapy is being used in a variety of schools (Seidel, 2011) and clinical settings (O'Brien, 2012; Tyson, 2012). Its use is based on the recognition that Hip Hop offers a more accessible alternatives to other established art therapies and that Hip Hop techniques can transcend societal barriers. For example, in his work concerning Hip Hop cyphers as a form of group counselling, Levy (2018) notes that the population which engages with the cypher "face various barriers in regards to their access to adequate mental health care, and subsequently are often left with unaddressed forms of emotional distress and trauma." Lauren Gardner (2014) also speaks of Hip Hop's "transformative potential," noting that the cypher "is a space where a person can speak the same language and communicate their ideas regardless of their identity category or social position" (p. 18).

Hip Hop offers an alternative approach to that of other art therapies, and has been recognised to have physical benefits. For example, dance artists are beginning to use Hip Hop dance forms to teach movement skills to those with conditions that affect mobility. For instance, weekly "Popping for Parkinson's" classes took place in London in 2016, led by dancer Simone Sistarelli. These classes were specifically developed for individuals with young onset Parkinson's. Researchers Philip and Malein noted, in relation to these particular classes, how Popping demands remarkable control over participants' muscles and specific kinds of movements. Philip and Malein describe how, throughout the class, participants began to use these new skills in muscle control to combat physical symptoms of the disease, such as tremors (Philip & Malein, 2016).

Whilst the physical benefits of Hip Hop dance have been more well-researched, few studies fully address the emotional, social and psychological benefits that it can offer. However, scholars have discussed techniques which may be found in more than one of Hip Hop's art forms. For example, the cypher which is seen in both rap and Hip Hop dance. Levy, Emdin, and Adjapong (2018) conducted a study in using rap cyphers in a group counselling setting. They noted how other methods of creative therapy may not adequately serve young people of colour in urban populations, and have offered Hip Hop as an additional option. For example, they demonstrate how the rap cypher can help adolescents develop a sense of emotional validation (Levy et al., 2018, p. 104). One of my interests is in how this research on the rap cypher can be applied to the dance cypher, furthering investigations into what Hip Hop may offer to marginalised groups underserved by creative therapies.

This chapter aims to add further discussion to the burgeoning area of study that investigates the potential of Hip Hop dance in therapeutic settings. I will provide a brief overview of Hip Hop's potential to grant agency to a variety of client groups, and offer some new Hip Hop-based tasks that can be utilised in similar settings. The chapter will describe a series of case studies following the development of these workshops over an 18 month period between 2017 and 2018. I will focus on three Hip Hop-based techniques that I use to create dance and spoken word with workshop participants, namely "The Remix," the breaking concept of "no biting" and the Hip Hop cypher. These techniques will be discussed in relation to the work of feminist therapists and dance movement psychotherapists in order to establish connections between Hip Hop's creative methods and other therapeutic techniques. Additionally, I extend the observations of an urban educator (Emdin, 2016) and a b-boy/social worker (Leafloor, 2012) on Hip Hop cyphers to note specific benefits of using the cypher model with neurodiverse young adults.

INTRODUCING A HIP HOP AND DANCE THERAPY PROGRAMME

In my work as an independent dance facilitator in the UK, I run workshops that bring dance and spoken word together through a series of Hip Hop-based techniques. These workshops aim to give agency back to those who feel that they have lost it as a result of difficult life experiences such as domestic abuse, sexual violence and stroke or being registered "disabled" in an arguably ableist society. A single workshop programme runs for between 8 and 12 weeks, and the sessions are delivered in a setting familiar to the participants. Sessions usually last for 1.5 hours, and participants work towards creating a collaborative piece of dance and spoken word which they may choose to present to an invited audience at the end of the programme, although this is not compulsory. Throughout the programme, participants take part in a series of Hip Hop-based creative tasks which enable them to generate words and movements that describe how they feel about their place in the world. Over time, participants are provided with the tools to turn these individual words and movements into coherent short pieces of dance and spoken word. My work has been described by the partners I work with (e.g., Dundee Women's Aid) as "therapeutic," and this has led me to investigate further how these workshops could provide an alternative to other art therapies.

Workshop Curriculum

The tasks that I use in these workshops have been developed organically through a process of trial and error, in tandem with theoretical perspectives in feminist therapy, Hip Hop education and dance movement psychotherapy. I keep regular journals which note how participants from different backgrounds respond to the different tasks, and this allows me to assess which techniques are most beneficial for each client group. The techniques that are discussed here are those which have had the most positive responses from participants. The observations made throughout this chapter are based on conversations with participants in the workshops, as well as via feedback forms completed by those involved.

I use the term "agency" to describe what these workshops offer participants. It is a term that is used frequently by psychologists such as Bandura (2006) and

Moore, who defines agency as a "feeling of control over actions and their consequences" (Moore, 2016). This definition is relevant to the workshops I deliver, given that my participants often feel that other people (or society at large) make life decisions for them, and as a result, they feel a lack of control over their own lives. The lack of confidence in the validity of their own opinions in their decision-making processes can lead to participants' sensing a loss of agency in their own lives. This can manifest itself in different ways. In the case of survivors of sexual violence, for example, agency has been taken away from these individuals as their lack of consent has been ignored by those who abused them. Feminist therapist Bonnie Burstow (1992) specifically talks about the importance of ensuring that survivors of all kinds of gender violence are able to make their own decisions about their journey in counselling and therapy. It is this sense of agency which I believe provides Hip Hop with its therapeutic potential.

The notion of agency has been discussed at length in counselling and therapeutic contexts. Hoener et al. discuss "clients as active participants in therapy" (p. 67). Their 2012 study involved interviewing 11 participants about their experiences of therapy, all of which spoke of the importance of agency in the therapeutic process, as it provided them with "positive feelings of personal accomplishment and empowerment" (Hoener et al., 2012, p. 79). Similarly, Gibson and Cartwright (2013) interviewed 22 young people aged 16–18 about their school counselling experience. Participants saw their own agency as "central to the change process" in counselling contexts. This research suggests that regaining a sense of agency forms a critical part of the therapeutic process, and is something which I believe Hip Hop can provide.

Please note that where feminist therapies or dance movement psychotherapy are referenced, it is not to claim that Hip Hop in this form is therapy, rather that its ability to provide a sense of agency suggests that there is therapeutic potential which should be researched further. I am not a therapist, rather an artist with an interest in the therapeutic applications of the work that I do. I believe that the discussion of established therapy and counselling practices can illuminate similarities between their approach, and that of the Hip Hop-based techniques I use in dance and spoken word, suggesting that Hip Hop can be used either in tandem with other therapeutic practices, or as an alternative to them.

Workshop Theory

This section will discuss theories which I have applied to my workshops in Hip Hop dance and spoken word: the theories of feminist therapy, dance movement psychotherapy and Hip Hop education.

Hip Hop and Feminist Therapy. Feminist therapy is based on the position that Western society is patriarchal in nature, and that modern psychiatry is equally patriarchal. Feminist therapists argue that women's psychological and emotional responses are pathologised as mental illness, whereby a woman feels a particular way because something is *wrong* with her, rather than acknowledging that her feelings may be a valid and completely normal response to difficult female-specific life experiences such as institutional sexism, sexual harassment, rape and domestic abuse (Burstow, 1992, p. 21).

Feminist therapists maintain that a woman's feelings cannot simply be "diagnosed" as some form of mental illness without understanding her background and how that may have affected her well-being. Veltre and Hadley (2012), who explored the use of a Hip Hop Feminist approach to music therapy with adolescent females, considered this further; noting that by situating the therapeutic process around the consent of the client, feminist therapists aim to restore any agency that has been stripped from that individual. Feminist therapist also emphasises the importance of client's decision-making in the therapeutic process, particularly when working with survivors of gender violence (Burstow, 1992). Using the therapeutic process to enable survivors to begin making their own decisions channels the importance of consent in working with this group. I use such a decision-making process in workshops with survivors of gender violence through a Hip Hop-based technique called "The Remix," which asks participants to make decisions in order to create a short performance of dance and spoken word. This technique will be discussed in more detail later.

Hip Hop Dance and Dance Movement Psychotherapy. Throughout my research in this area, I have noted various similarities between the practice of Dance Movement Psychotherapy, and a variety of Hip Hop-based techniques. A similarity which has stood out most for me can be found in the breaking concept of "no biting." This idea demands that dancers do not copy the movements of another dancer. If they are to learn how to do a head spin, for example, they must adapt the movement to fit their own body, and to make it their own. Whilst the ethos of "'no biting" provides dancers agency through encouraging them to make each movement unique to them, dance movement psychotherapists such as Chodorow and Schoop have used similar movement tasks which encourage clients to "[d]o it in your own way" (Chodorow, 1991, p. 19).

Chodorow describes a variety of movement tasks which DMP pioneer Trudi Schoop offered to her patients. Schoop would offer a movement to the room, and the participants would be instructed to do the movement in their own way. Schoop's instructions allowed each participant to tap into a particular movement, but by using their own natural movement style to do so. A participant may not identify exactly with the movement that the therapist is performing, or with those they see others performing around them, but they are invited to create their own, within a framework. The structure offered by the original movement allows participants to feel a part of the group, whilst performing the movement in their own way encourages them to address their own individuality within the structure that the movement offers. I argue that the structure offered by the movement vocabulary of Hip Hop dance offers a framework with which an individual can identify, but gives that person the freedom to explore their own movement style within that framework.

Hip Hop Education. A fundamental element of Hip Hop is the cypher. For those unfamiliar with this concept, the cypher involves Hip Hop dancers or rappers/ spoken word artists standing in a circle. Participants move into the middle of the circle and improvise for a short time. Rules of the cypher include offering unfailing support through claps and cheers of encouragement directed at those who step into the centre, regardless of whether they "mess up" or not. In his study of using breaking to tackle mental health issues in Canada's Arctic and First Nation communities, b-boy and social worker Stephen Leafloor describes the breaking cypher as "cognitive therapy," and as an "equaliser," noting that everyone is supported in a cypher, even if they get the moves "wrong" (Leafloor, 2012, p. 138).

Urban education specialist, Emdin, has experimented extensively with the potential of the Hip Hop cypher has for working in urban education settings. He makes particular reference to how the cypher provides a platform for exploring shared neoindigeneity as a group of people often considered outsiders in society (Emdin, 2016, p. 63). This notion of neoindigeneity became very relevant for me when working with groups of young people with special educational needs. As Emdin states, the cypher provides a shared platform which allows individuals to describe the realities of their lives; realities which often differ considerably from those of others. This is pertinent to the case of young people on the autistic spectrum and those with a variety of learning and physical disabilities as their realities are often not taken into consideration by wider society. Buildings and institutions are not always adapted to suit the needs of these individuals and, as a result, they can be left feeling as if their realities are less important than those of others.

However, as noted by Emdin (2016), the cypher can offer an opportunity for such individuals to share their feelings with others who may have experienced a similar situation.

HIP HOP TECHNIQUES IN PRACTICE

I have established the theories that have influenced my workshops in Hip Hop dance and spoken word, and now turn to the individual Hip Hop-based techniques that I use: "The Remix," the breaking concept of "no biting" and the Hip Hop cypher. In this section, I describe these techniques and their results in working with survivors of gender violence, stroke survivors and neurodiverse young adults, respectively.

The Remix

For some, the idea of writing a rap or a piece of spoken word, or choreographing a Hip Hop dance performance can be particularly daunting prospects and, therefore, may not seem an appropriate starting point to help clients address difficult life experiences. However, starting by working with Hip Hop's creation processes, rather than focusing on an end product such as a rap or dance, is one way to resolve this difficulty. I have found that Hip Hop's remix or sampling aesthetic can be used to inspire tasks which allow participants to embark on a journey in creating a rap or dance at a much slower pace. These tasks are inspired by Hip Hop's bricolage approach to creating, in that Hip Hop DJs, dancers, rappers and producers have historically taken elements of existing songs, dance forms and lyrics and re-fashioned them into something new. Using Hip Hop to create in this way means that clients do not have the daunting task of starting from scratch in the creation of their dance and spoken word, but can adapt works that already exist in order to express themselves.

In early 2017, I began facilitating a programme of dance and spoken word workshops with women recovering from gender violence in Dundee, in partnership with Dundee Women's Aid and the Women's Rape and Sexual Abuse Centre for Dundee and Angus. I found the theories of feminist therapists such as Burstow (1992) most helpful in informing workshops with female survivors of gender violence. Through the development of a process called "The Remix," I have begun to address the decision-making aspect of feminist therapy. The Remix is a democratic process for developing dance and spoken word work with communities who may know nothing about either art form or about Hip Hop culture. It asks them to move around words and movements from existing performances in order to express their own opinions on the subjects explored within these works.

There are various places to begin in the process which The Remix offers as a creation method. The option that I follow in a session depends on how the participants are feeling in that moment. The less confident that the participants feel, the more I focus on enabling them to re-work existing pieces of dance and spoken word. For example, I may bring in a set of lyrics which we read through together. After discussing initial thoughts on the words, we start to work through the lyrics line by line. Participants are given two options to consider how these lyrics can be adapted to fit their own experiences: (1) to delete individual words and/or whole lines which they do not feel apply to them, and (2) to re-write sentences which go some way to describing their feelings, but do not quite achieve this. I find that this method opens up discussions around participants' experiences, without feeling that they have to find the words to fully describe it themselves; they can choose to agree or disagree with the lyrics that they are presented with, and use those decisions to begin to create their own piece of spoken word.

A second version of this creation method involves generating a series of random words before applying The Remix approach, and is often used when participants are feeling more confident. This process begins by choosing a series of words relating to a theme. For example, participants in the sessions at Dundee Women's Aid collectively chose the theme of "journeys" as they felt that this best expressed their collective recovery stories, many of which were still in progress. Each word is written on a small piece of card, and I invite participants to move these words around to create a short text work. One set of words can be moved around infinitely, each new edition creating a "remix" of the previous one. I then give the participants tasks to turn the text into spoken word. I ask them to think about where a performer might take a breath in order to create double meanings and to draw attention to particular words or phrases. I also initiate discussions around the speed at which the words are performed, and the reasons for this; do they want to speak faster to give their audience a sense of urgency? Do they want to speak more slowly to express the idea of time passing slowly?

In each of these tasks, there is a focus on the participants making decisions for themselves. We discuss the reasons for making these decisions. For example, upon removing a word or phrase from an existing set of lyrics, we discuss why they feel that particular sentiment applies to them, or how they interpret what the lyricist means and why they do not agree with the opinions expressed in the original rap. In the case of the second task, we might consider why a participant chose to take a breath at a particular moment in the performance of the words; what is she trying to draw people's attention to and why? These decisions are informed by the lived experiences of the participants, and so the spoken word that is created becomes autobiographical, as are the lyrics of many rap artists. However, rather than simply writing an autobiographical rap, the process of The Remix demands that participants make informed choices about how they express their spoken word.

The women's creative decision-making in the writing of their spoken word, a process which directly relates to their experiences of gender violence, begins to restore agency in these women. Upon finishing their piece of spoken word, participants have described feelings of being in control of their creative process. For these women, this feeling of being in control is often a rare moment. Through these decisions, the participant actively shapes her own therapy, which echoes the feminist approach to therapeutic practices that Burstow (1992) and Veltre and Hadley (2012) refer to.

Throughout these workshop programmes, the participants and I engage in another decision-making process; to collectively create choreography that will accompany the spoken word performances. Keeping in line with Burstow's notion of decision-making processes in feminist therapy, I once again offer the participants a variety of different options. Firstly, they can choose to "remix" a piece of choreography that I prepared and presented to them. Alternatively, I suggest two movements which might accompany a particular word or phrase from their own spoken word, and they vote on which movement they prefer. Simply by offering those women the chance to cast their votes on the movements which they want to accompany the words, I am saying "I care what you think." This is a sentiment that many of the women I work with report that they have never experienced before. One participant in the 2017 workshops noted:

> It was so empowering and made me feel like my opinion and ideas really mattered. This does not usually happen to me where I feel respected and part of something (Anon., *Feedback on dance and spoken word workshop* [email], personal communication, April 3, 2017).

By gaining confidence through the use of The Remix concept, participants gradually feel more comfortable in their own creative process and, in turn, their own decision-making process. For the women I work with, this process gives them their voices back and begins to allow them to reconnect with their bodies after having been silenced for too long.

By combining Hip Hop with feminist approaches to therapy, The Remix allows women who have experienced gender violence to regain agency. Although the current sample size in this instance is rather small (11 women benefited from the Dundee-based programme), I advocate further research into how this technique can be used to enable such clients to gain a sense of control over their life experiences, and to help them effectively deal with issues of consent and decision making in a creative way.

Workshops to date suggest that The Remix is a powerful method for helping these women deal with their difficult life experiences, just as rappers do through their work. Hip Hop has arguably always been a response to oppression (Chang, 2005) and its combination with feminist approaches to therapy demonstrate another way in which it might respond to the injustices in society.

No Biting

The case of a particular participant in the artifact's dance and spoken word workshops provide an example of how the concept of "no biting" can help to provide agency to clients. In early 2018, I worked with Tayside Healthcare Arts Trust in Scotland to deliver a series of 10 dance and spoken word workshops to a group of 6 older people recovering from experiences of stroke. John* was a stroke survivor who used to dance the Jive before his stroke, and found himself unable to do so afterwards. John learnt the concept of "no biting" in one of my workshops, alongside learning two Hip Hop dance movements; top rocks and a lazy boi spin. "No biting" was of particular relevance for the lazy boi spin as stroke survivors find that their balance is affected by their ordeal, and so spins can present difficulties.

With each participant, I worked through how they might be able to adapt the lazy boi spin to make the movement comfortable for their bodies to perform. It was encouraged that this movement be fluid; that is, that the participants wouldn't necessarily always perform the movement in this way, as they could try out new ways of performing it as their balance improved throughout their recovery. After being involved in these workshops, John took on the concept of "no biting" in order to adapt more movements for his post-stroke body, and teach himself to dance the Jive again.

Hip Hop's emphasis on individuality, as represented through the breaking concept of "no biting," presents the participants of these workshops with another opportunity to exercise agency, in that they are placed in control of their own physical recovery. By adapting movements to fit their body, they better understand their own limitations and what they need to focus on in order to potentially gain a full physical recovery from their stroke. "No biting" becomes a tool through which they can experiment with coordination and muscle weakness. In addition, "no biting" offers a sense of agency which extends beyond a physical tool for exploring movement possibilities in that it does not make excuses for a person not being able to perform a movement in a particular way.

There is a fundamental difference between telling a participant that it is okay if they get a movement "wrong" and telling them that there is no "wrong" movement. The latter suggests that the participant is always making progress, whilst the former implies that the facilitator is making concessions for them. This can have great psychological and emotional benefits in that participants feel a sense of achievement, no matter how they perform a particular movement. In fact, 100% of participants on this particular programme reported increased benefits in mood, confidence, communication and socialisation, with 80% also reporting an increase in communication skills. These improvements were also observed by healthcare partners in the project and suggest that they felt better equipped to express themselves as a direct result of the workshops (Tayside Healthcare Arts Trust, 2018).

The breaking concept of "no biting" can be compared to Dance Movement Psychotherapy in that it works with movements that are already there. This comparison is useful in that it illuminates the therapeutic potential of Hip Hop dance forms. Hip Hop dance concepts such as "no biting" provide agency in the form over control of a client's own recovery. In the case of stroke survivors, clients can use this concept to regain abilities in other areas of their life, such as re-teaching themselves skills that they have lost as a result of their stroke.

The Hip Hop Cypher

In my workshops, I use the model of the Hip Hop cypher to generate both dance and spoken word because I find that it encourages participants to generate spontaneous ideas without fear of getting anything "wrong." In early 2018, I worked with INFORM Theatre, a group of young adults with learning disabilities based at Dundee Rep Theatre in Scotland in early 2018. Together we created a new performance of dance and spoken word about disability hate crime, developed by those who are deemed "disabled" by society, instead of organisations which label them as such. With this group, I used the Hip Hop cypher as a platform for generating dance and spoken word. In line with Leafloor's (2012) work, everyone who offered something into the cypher was supported by their peers, regardless of how "well" they executed the words or movements which they offered. In this case, the unique bodies of these young people were celebrated; their bodies often do not move in the ways that others do, but in the cypher there were no "right" or "wrong" movements. In fact, these young people both spoke and moved in ways which wider society does not deem "normal."

For example, one participant, Robert*, had a stutter. At the beginning of the project, he was rather shy and very aware of his stutter, and so didn't speak very much at all. However, as the project developed he gained confidence in this area, through the use of the cypher. When offering improvised spoken word in the cypher, he was supported by his peers, which gave him the assurance he needed to continue. His stutter was validated, as well as the emotional content he offered to the group. His community supported him in speaking by giving him the time he needed to say all that he wanted to. In other areas of society, someone might try to be helpful by finishing this young man's sentences for him. This does not happen in the cypher; each participant is given the time they need to finish what they are saying or how they are moving. This ethos helped Robert to feel that his stutter is not a hindrance, but something that is a part of him, and should be a celebrated element of his individuality. The cypher began to restore his agency in that he felt encouraged to speak and felt a sense of achievement when he managed to complete the spoken word which he was performing.

INFORM Theatre used the cypher, and it's potential to celebrate the group's individualities in order to create their final performance. In this performance, participants reclaimed their agency by asking society not to think of them as "disabled," rather to consider them "differently abled"; as individuals who can offer society a different perspective.

CONCLUSION

The Hip Hop-based techniques described in this chapter—The Remix, the concept of "no biting" and the Hip Hop cypher—have provided my workshop participants with a sense of agency in a variety of different ways, and therefore could be combined to inform the beginnings of a new therapeutic process. The similarities between these techniques and the approaches of feminist therapy and dance movement psychotherapy begin to demonstrate Hip Hop's therapeutic potential in working with survivors of gender violence, and with those with long-term health conditions. The burgeoning movement of Hip Hop Education and Hip Hop counselling is beginning to expand this further; however, much is still to be done in this area, particularly around how Hip Hop dance can offer new techniques for use in therapeutic contexts.

Given the many avenues still to explore in how Hip Hop dance and spoken word can restore agency to marginalised groups and those who have survived difficult life experiences, it feels odd to end this chapter with a conclusion, as our work is far from done. Instead, I'd like to end with a plea to help us make the next steps and to advocate for Hip Hop's therapeutic potential on a wider level. To do this, let's draw on another Hip Hop concept: "each one, teach one." This is another message that is used by the breaking community; the idea that if each b-boy or b-girl pass their knowledge and skills on to one other person, the art form will continue to thrive. I want to ask you to do the same with the knowledge and insights offered in this book so that more people around the world can gain access to Hip Hop's healing potential. Spread the word about what you find here, and pass it on.

*Names of participants have been changed to protect their anonymity

REFERENCES

Bandura, A. (2006). Toward a psychology of human agency: Pathways and reflections. *Perspectives on Psychological Science, 1*(2), 164–180.

Bungay, H., & Vella-Burrows, T. (2013). The effects of participating in creative activities on the health and well-being of children and young people: A rapid review of the literature. *Perspectives in Public Health, 133*(1), 44–52.

Burstow, B. (1992). *Radical feminist therapy: Working in the context of violence.* Newbury Park, CA: Sage.

Chang, J. (2005). *Can't stop, won't stop: A history of the hip-hop generation.* Great Britain: Ebury Press.

Chodorow, J. (1991). *Dance therapy & depth psychology: The moving imagination.* London, England/New York, NY: Routledge.

Di Blasio, P., Camisasca, E., Caravita, S., Carla, S., Ionio, C., Milani, L., & Valtolina, G.G. (2015). The effects of expressive writing on postpartum depression and posttraumatic stress symptoms. *Psychological Reports, 117*(3), 856–882.

Emdin, C. (2016). *For white folks who teach in the hood... and the rest of y'all too: Reality pedagogy and urban education.* Boston, MA: Beacon Press.

Gardner, L.M. (2014). "We either mover or petrify": Transnational hip hop feminisms amongst hip hop dancers and graffiteros—A critical literature review [online]. In *GEMS (Gender, Education, Music, and Society), the on-line journal of GRIME (Gender Research in Music Education), 7*(4), 12–21. Retrieved 12 October, 2018, from https://ojs.library.queensu.ca/index.php/gems/issue/view/508.

Gibson, K., & Cartwright, C. (2013). Agency in young clients' narratives of counseling: "It's whatever you want to make of it." *Journal of Counseling Psychology, 60*(3), 340–352.

Hoener, C., Stiles, W.B., Luka, B.J., & Gordon, R.A. (2012). Client experiences of agency in therapy. In *Person-centred & experiential psychotherapies* (pp. 64–82). Abingdon, England: Taylor & Francis Ltd.

Leafloor, S. (2012). Therapeutic outreach through bboying (break dancing) in Canada's arctic and first nations communities: Social work through hip-hop. In S. Hadley & G. Yancy (Eds.), *Therapeutic uses of rap and hip-hop* (pp. 129–138). New York, NY/London, England: Routledge.

Levy, I. (2018). Aligning community defined practice with evidence based group counseling: The hip-hop cypher as group counseling. In C. Emdin & E. Adjapong (Eds.), *#hipHopEd: The compilation on hip-hop education. Volume 1: Hip-hop as education, philosophy, and practice* (pp. 170–180). Leiden: Brill Sense.

Levy, I., Emdin, C., & Adjapong, E.S. (2018). Hip-hop cypher in group work. In A. Malekoff (Ed.), *Social work with groups* (Group work and the arts, Vol. 41, No. 1–2, pp. 103–110). London, England: Routledge.

Moore, J.W. (2016). What is the sense of agency and why does it matter? *Frontiers in Psychology, 7* [online]. Retrieved 17 October, 2018, from https://www.ncbi.nlm.nih.gov/pmc/articles/PMC5002400/

O'Brien, E. (2012). "Morphine mamma": Creating original songs using rap with women and cancer. In S. Hadley & G. Yancy (Eds.), *Therapeutic uses of rap and hip-hop* (pp. 337–352). New York, NY/London, England: Routledge.

Papagiannaki, A., & Shinebourne, P. (2016). The contribution of creative art therapies to promoting mental health: Using interpretive phenomenological analysis to study therapists' understanding of working with self-stigmatisation. *The Arts in Psychotherapy, 50*(1), 66–74.

Philip, K., & Malein, F. (2016). *Popping for Parkinson's* [online]. Retrieved 13 May, 2018, from https://www.communitydance.org.uk/DB/animated-library/popping-for-parkinsons?ed=35176

Rose, T. (2008). *The hip hop wars: What we talk about when we talk about hip hop and why it matters.* New York, NY: Basic Books.

Seidel, S. (2011). *Hip hop genius: Remixing high school education.* Lanham, MD: Rowman & Littlefield Education.

Tayside Healthcare Arts Trust (2018). *ST/ART project programme summary report year 2017–2018. Programme: Our flow with dundee stroke exercise club.* Dundee, Scotland: Tayside Healthcare Arts Trust.

Tyson, E.H. (2012). Hip-hop healing: Rap music in grief therapy with an african american adolescent male. In S. Hadley and G. Yancy (Eds.), *Therapeutic uses of rap and hip-hop* (pp. 293–305). New York, NY/London, England: Routledge.

Veltre, V.J., & Hadley, S. (2012). It's bigger than hip-hop: A hip-hop feminist approach to music therapy with adolescent females. In S. Hadley & G. Yancy (Eds.), *Therapeutic uses of rap and hip-hop* (pp. 79–98). New York, NY/London, England: Routledge.

CHAPTER EIGHT

Building Character through Hip Hop

JANINE BROWN

@MsBBrilliance

As if my highly melanated complexion was not the obvious clue, I possessed a laundry list of what I now call distinctions. In my young adult years, I was conditioned to reject my intrinsic mode of expression and demeanor as means to gain acceptance and be successful. Though I am from Jersey, it was said that I had a New York accent. Add a pinch of Black vernacular English that lacked "-ing" suffixes; sprinkle a couple of overemphasized vowel sounds; blend in particular phrases that was accompanied by an undeniable tough exterior and you have the perfect antithesis of the majority.

My undergraduate years at Rutgers did not prepare me for the sore reminder of otherness that greeted me as I entered a post baccalaureate Journalism program at the University of Iowa. I had hopes and aspirations of becoming a on-air news personality, my confidence dissipated and insecurity arose because of those attributes that were ingrained in my identity. A therapist dubbed it as classic performance anxiety—the fear of speaking in front of what I assumed to be a judgmental audience. I practiced breathing and grounding techniques, I imitated the speech of my white counterparts, and even visited a dialect coach until eventually, I dismissed the idea of being on television altogether.

In retrospect, a therapist was helpful to some degree, but it did not address the larger issue at hand. Ultimately, what I needed was a professor to validate the greatness within my uniqueness. What I needed was an advisor to allow the natural elements of my identity to shine rather than fade. Instead, I was subjected to educators who, through blind convention, promoted assimilation rather than acculturation. Instead, I was subjected to educators who unknowingly assisted in the death of a dream by not acknowledging my social assets.

Cultural capital encompasses the identifiers such as mannerisms, dress, beliefs, and values that advance a person's self-worth (Goldenberg, 2014). My experience, the feeling of inadequacy, is not uncommon for students of non dominant culture. Being subjected to the process of traditional schooling (dominant culture) can prove to be detrimental to the social and emotional development of an individual. Some of the feelings include feeling like their cultural values were unwelcomed and discounted (Goldenberg, 2014). Hip hop education can alleviate the feelings of exclusivity because it [hip hop] is hardwired to learning potential and identities; and also allows them to see their culture affirmed and recognized" (Love, 2015, p. 109). Imagine if knowledge of self, in collaboration with character education, were at the core of instruction. The result may have been different. The qualities that I viewed as hindrances in academia and mainstream media could have very well been the same assets that propelled my success in the field. Developing confidence and esteem during my schooling could have made the difference between advancing and quitting. This is the crux of why hip-hip education is crucial in youth development and success—to challenge this disservice of unjust assimilation; combat inequities and ultimately give value to their cultural capital.

The goal of the #HipHopEd movement is to "disrupt the oppressive structures of schools and schooling for marginalized youth through a reframing of hip hop in the public sphere" (Adjapong & Emdin, 2018, p. 1). To legitimize hip hop pedagogy further, it is important to note that hip hop scholarship "has become relevant to the field of education in that teachers are centering rap lyrical texts often in the name of culturally responsive teaching and critical pedagogy, to empower marginalized groups, teach academic skills, and educate students about how aspects of their lives are subject to manipulation and control" (Petchauer, 2009, p. 947).

As a Language Arts teacher, the utilization of hip hop theory and music was paramount in terms of texts chosen, increasing student engagement and achievement on standardized tests. As I transitioned into a new role as a Crisis Intervention Teacher (CIT), I discovered that the use of hip hop is still highly advantageous in handling student crises; understanding the root causes of those issues; and building character to prevent some of those crises. While consuming the music, I often hear lyrics that are reminiscent of the experiences my youth endure and it became fitting to use excerpts of the music as means to connect and initiate and facilitate discussion. However there is very little discussion about its influence on building character and discipline practices. Therefore, this chapter will explore the unique social emotional and cultural needs of marginalized populations; and how hip hop pedagogy can be utilized to enhance and strengthen character education curriculums and promote the reconceptualization of discipline practices.

BACKGROUND ON CHARACTER EDUCATION

The idea of character education is not a new one. Dating back to the 19th century, what we call character education today was once described as moral education and conceptualized from the French education system. It arose from the perceived need for morality to be taught in schools (Watz, 2011). According to Watz's (2011) historical overview, Horace Mann, a prominent character education advocate in the 19th century, believed that teaching character was important to the education process and how he ascertained that without morality, the character of students would not fully develop. The lack of morality was theorized to lead to undesirable behavior and poor academic standing (Watz, 2011). This basic principle of character education continued into the 20th century with John Dewey, education reformist, as a major proponent. In the 20th century it was believed that "the establishing of character is a comprehensive aim of school instruction and discipline" (Tatman, Edmonson, & Slate, 2009, para 2). Furthermore, he defined a true educational environment as academic and character rich with the expectation of improving social conditions (White, 2015).

CRITIQUE OF CHARACTER EDUCATION

Despite its well intentioned purpose, character education has fought to be a permanent fixture in public schools. Character education has been described as "a wave that the tide has carried in and out due to societal pressures such as political, religious, or corporate influences" (Watz, 2011, p. 44). This metaphorical wave is used to describe a bevy of issues. First, much of the scope of criticism relates to the manner in which it is implemented. Research suggests that character education could be ineffective because of its focus on students irrespective of their cultural capital dismissing their "social-cultural contexts such as gender, ethnicity and power relations" (Walker, Roberts, & Kristjansson, 2015, p. 85). Furthermore, those that challenge or are skeptical of the effectiveness of character education address the difficulty that teachers have in finding balance between teaching academic and character content (Baehr, 2017). Additionally, researcher, Brian White, explored historical critiques of character education and found that moral/character education could be more valid if it weren't for a "dogged insistence upon conformity" (White, 2015, p. 135).

It is important to note that character education has evolved into a broad umbrella with various components that include Social Emotional Learning (SEL); building skills, virtues, performance values; and improving school climate/culture. While many SEL programs are well founded, many SEL and behavioral programs do not successfully address life situations experienced by urban African American children (Graves et al., 2017) and consequently, culturally adapting current existing SEL programs may help students identify, grasp, maintain and generalize the curriculum material in a more efficient manner (Graves et al.).

If hip hop pedagogy can be used to address challenges of character education, then it can most certainly be used to strengthen SEL especially because culturally responsive programing is particularly necessary when assisting youth in exploring emotional difficulties that hinder their development (Griner & Stewart, 2012).

SOCIAL EMOTIONAL LEARNING: A RESPONSE TO TRAUMA AND NEGATIVE BEHAVIOR

In recent years, character education has regained popularity in public schools in response to violence and tragedies in schools (Watz, 2011). Further, research suggests that SEL, an extremely vital piece of character education, can specifically help address poor behavior in public schools (Terrasi & Galarce, 2017). SEL can be described as an overarching theme that involves:

> acquiring and effectively applying the knowledge, attitudes, and skills to understand and manage emotions, set and achieve positive goals, feel and show empathy for others, establish and maintain positive relationships, and make responsible decisions. Schools can help prevent or reduce many different risky behaviors (e.g., drug use, violence, bullying, and dropping out) when they engage in multiyear, integrated efforts to develop students' social and emotional skills. (Weissberg & Cascarino, 2013, p. 3)

In other words, we are not born with all the skills necessary to have positive life outcomes. Rather, they need to be taught and schools share part of that responsibility. Rapper J. Cole highlighted the limitations of our emotions at birth on the intro to his album, KOD (Kids on Drugs). Over a melodic jazz saxophone a tranquilizing voice whispers:

> A newborn baby has two primary modes of communication: laughter, which says I love this...or crying which says this frightens me, I'm in pain. There are many ways to deal with this pain. (Cole, 2018, Intro, KOD)

This observation is validated by the writing of Eric Jensen (2010) in his book, *Teaching with Poverty in Mind*. Jensen (2010) discusses how particular interactions are necessary before the age of three in order to have healthy relationships. He explains the importance of the attunement process between birth and 2 years old. Attunement is a process of harmonious reciprocal interaction for 10–20 hours a week. It is believed that this helps to develop gratitude, empathy and forgiveness (Jensen, 2010). The sad reality is that for many in urban communities, the attunement/attachment process can be interrupted or inadequate due to stressful circumstances. Russ Sojourner, former director of the Character Education Partnership, a coalition of character education advocates, affirms this notion and the importance of SEL taking place in the school setting. He writes: "the family home provides deep emotional nourishment for the child, but rarely does this happen in a typical U.S. household these days. In a day when children are emotionally malnourished, much rides on the adults they see everyday—educators" (Sojourner, 2014, p. 70). This couldn't be more true. As a CIT, I engage daily with children who struggle with managing their emotions. These difficulties manifest as chronic behavioral concerns that are not conducive to an effective learning environment. In conferencing with the caregivers of those children, past and present traumas are often revealed.

Dr. Maurice Elias, co-director of the Rutgers University Social Emotional Learning Lab, has conducted extensive field work and inquiry on the implementation of SEL (Elias, 2009,2013; Elias & Leverett, 2011); the effects trauma can have on learning; and how effective it can be for students dealing with trauma.

> Conditions such as these (traumas) strongly erode the capabilities of students to concentrate on academic tasks, primarily because they engender strong emotions such as fear, anxiety, boredom, depression, despair, upset, and rage that are incompatible with effective learning and retention. For students to learn effectively in spite of such influences requires skills in emotion recognition and management and sound coping and problem solving skills. (Elias & Leverett, 2011, p. 31)

For urban students of color, SEL programming is vital to combating historic inequities. Black males are disproportionately placed in special education class for emotional-behavioral disorders (Graves et al., 2017). In addition, students of color, particularly in urban schools, generally face high incidences of disciplinary actions, suspensions, and expulsions (Boutte, 2012). Many progressive education theorists contend that culturally responsive teaching is key in remedying inequities; while researchers like Dr. Elias advocate for SEL. Both schools of thought have been proven to produce desirable outcomes independently. Dr. Elias argues that the advancement of urban children is dependent upon schools' willingness to attend to students' social emotional and character development (Elias & Leverett, 2011). Conversely, research shows that the cultures of students of color are missing in urban schools (Boutte, 2012). I argue that a convergence of the two approaches to teaching; culturally responsive SEL programs will yield a comprehensive result that will address and include the cultural capital of students; while responding to their adverse childhood experiences to achieve desirable outcomes.

CONSTRUCTING RESILIENCE: BEGIN WITH THE END IN MIND

SEL is a means to an end. That end goal varies depending on one's frame of reference, but for adolescents of color that goal is almost always to survive and thrive based on historical disconnect between diverse students and academic institutions (Griner & Stewart, 2012). Put simply, to be resilient in the face of adversity and trauma. Most character education and SEL curriculums advocate for the promotion of resilience as a direct response to trauma because "learning can undo trauma" (Terrasi & DeGalarce, 2017). The idea is that practicing certain coping mechanism such as regulating their emotions and communication skills, it can allow for students to push through barriers.

> every child capable of developing a resilient mindset will be able to deal more effectively with stress and pressure, to cope with everyday challenges, to bounce back from disappointments, adversity, and trauma, to develop clear and realistic goals, to solve problems, to relate comfortably with others, and to treat oneself and others with respect. (Goldstein & Brooks, 2013, p. 3)

Developing resilience is dependent upon several factors including:

> individual's capacity to overcome life challenges as it is the capacity of the child's informal and formal social networks to facilitate positive development under stress (Obrist, Pfeiffer, & Henley, 2010; Ungar, 2011c). This social ecological understanding of resilience implicates those who control the resources that facilitate psychological well-being in the proximal processes (e.g., making education accessible; promoting a sense of belonging in one's community; facilitating attachment to a caregiver; affirmation of self-worth) associated with positive development in contexts of adversity. (Ungar, 2013, p. 255)

With that being said, it is pertinent for educators to be a conduit for resilience to flourish.

Authors of Fostering Resilient Learners recognize that children are resilient (Hall & Sourers, 2016). They define resilience as the ability and inner strength to rebound from challenges. They also posit that it (resilience) can be learned and practiced and not genetic. While much of the discourse around interventions for dealing with trauma in children relates to the need to build, teach and promote resilience, it is equally important to acknowledge that resilience is cultural capital for hip hop urban children. Within dominant culture, resilience is viewed as overcoming trauma and the effect is success, but within the non dominant culture it can be viewed as having the grit to survive insurmountable circumstances. This is evidenced by the second grader who doesn't sleep well because his parents are arguing; or the fifth grader who manages to complete her homework every night despite having to care for a younger siblings after school. The cultural capital resilience manifests as the eighth grader who writes expressive poetry about the incident she has endured instead of engaging in other unhealthy habits.

On a recent visit to the African American Museum, a particular quote resonated with me and reminded me of the work educators do daily. "While many souls were lost during the Middle Passage, those who survived did so through courage, will and strength of the human spirit." Having the background knowledge and understanding the stressors (traumas) our students face culturally, socially and emotionally, it is the job of the educator to give credence to the non dominant idea of resilience. This is accomplished by creating relationships and safe spaces for the trauma to be articulated (*courage*); validation of the *strength* to overcome those trials, and then we can move toward the desire to develop those secondary traits (*will of human spirit*) that are revered by character education experts to achieve success.

INCORPORATING HIP HOP

As evidenced in this commentary, character education is a necessary component in the overall development of youth. While it can serve as a preventive and reactive measure to address the social emotional needs of students; its true efficacy is dependent upon the level of cultural responsiveness with which it is implemented. Hip Hop is an ideal framework for cultural relevance given its emphasis on youth knowledge, cultural identity and capital and innate resilience.

Character Education Partnership provides an excellent framework for establishing character building programs that encompasses six prescribed performance values below. The inclusion of the hip hop elements, music, and culture can enrich the instruction because of its ability to connect to young people.

1. *Assigning work that matters:* Learn what students value. In some cases, they value toughness, they value success. They respect grit. What matters to your students? What are their traumas? What are their interest, gifts and talents? What artist and music do they like?

   Example: Activity 1: Hip Hop Storytelling/Narrative Writing

   The objective of this lesson was to listen to "Window Pain Outro" by J. Cole. The students were asked to make text to self connections by modeling a similar narrative to J. Cole. I created the following prompt to guide their thinking. In the song, J. Cole writes about traumatic childhood experiences, write about a time you experienced a traumatic situation. Be sure to include the who, what, when, where and why. How did you feel? What effects has it had on your life? I engaged in the activity as well to help create that safe space to share by writing about growing up with a mentally ill parent. After the youth produced their writing, I asked for volunteers to share out. Many similarities arose from the responses. Some students wrote about losing a loved one, witnessing an act of violence and experiencing divorce of parents. We then discussed the effects it had on us and charted coping strategies such as listening to music, journaling, and talking to a school counselor. In the end, students were given a platform to find and use their voice to reflect on their experiences; as well as helped me to get to know and understand the students I served.

2. *Develop thinking dispositions:* Encourage students to question, challenge or acquiesce.

Example: Activity 2: Fact or Fiction

The objective was to compare and contrast Tekashi 6ix9ine's lyrics to a statement he gave through his lawyer. I asked the students to draw an informed conclusion about the rapper based on his music persona and real life. I conducted a brief debate about the rapper's innocence or guilt in which students used reliable media sources to provide evidence to support their ideas. It was interesting to see students change their initial opinion of the rapper and watch others remain convicted in their belief. Despite their assessment, the goal was achieved because most left the lesson questioning and being more critical of media they consume.

3. *Provide models of excellence:* Model, produce and provide exemplars of expectations around the room. It could be posters, writing, photos, etc.

4. *Create a culture of excellence:* Cultivate a classroom where success is the normalize.

Example: Activity 3: Pathways to Success

Students were asked to identify at least five successful internet/YouTube rapper or content creators who created their own lane and platform for their music. Students were then placed in groups to discuss their lists and talk about the steps taken to get to the next level. Students then created flowcharts that mapped out their intended pathway to success. Some students struggled with this activity which was expected because many never gave it thought, while others quickly devised their plan. The purpose was to create and foster a mindset that views excellence in different ways and promote the various ways to achieve it.

5. *Growth mindset with emphasis on effort:* Step outside comfort zone for the benefit of students.

Example: Activity 4: Timeline

Cardi B's rise to fame is one to commended. Her song Get Up 10 is a realistic account of survival and overcoming obstacles to achieve goals. In recent commentary, Dr. Chris Emdin, founder of #hiphoped, notes how educators often make the mistake of only focusing on survival and not thriving (Emdin, 2016). Well, not only did she survive—through the strip club and social media; we were privileged to watch as she thrived by breaking records to become not just a hip hop star, but an international star. Because of her relatability, I created a lesson plan with the objective of listening and reviewing "Get Up 10." Students were asked to highlight and discuss the challenges she overcame and then documented Cardi's rise on a timeline. With completed timelines, we examined the implications of her work ethic and how her image has evolved. This lesson was successful because of the popularity of the artist and served as an example of personal growth.

6. *Creating safe learning communities:* With all lesson plans it is extremely important to create safe learning communities. I accomplish this by demonstrating vulnerability. I always model and share my own story so in turn, students feel safe enough to tell theirs. This builds trust between teacher and students and also amongst classmates.

Keeping these performance values in mind when creating SEL and character building lessons strengthens its efficacy.

CONCLUSION

Long gone are the days where the teaching profession is simply about delivering content. That is no longer the nature of the job! Reform, in terms of teacher training, SEL and cultural responsiveness is imminent. Progressive educators and educactivist will eventually propose law amendments to require culturally relevant teaching and SEL. Much like the NJ Amistad Law, in which social studies teachers are mandated to include African American history—I foresee a shift in which teachers will be required to facilitate SEL and hip hop pedagogy will be offered as a strategy to engage learners. Some will champion it; others will be against it—citing it as just one more thing teachers have to do. However, if one is not willing to evolve in their teaching style and attempt innovative strategies and adapt to youth culture, it may be time for a new field.

Undeniably the goal of character education and SEL is to enhance and improve the lives of students. This in turn also positively affects school climate. Without a doubt schools are intended to provide safe and supportive learning environments. I argue that sound SEL and character education program coupled with hip hop education is a transformative combination that can and will alter education for the better for youth. Independent of each other, both conduits are necessary for students to be global contributors to society. The best aspect about both is that the premise is not about content, grades or tests. Both pedagogies focus on the whole student which will inevitably open up a pathway to academic success and achievement.

REFERENCES

Baehr, J. (2017). The varieties of character and some implications for character education. *Journal of youth and adolescence*, *46*(6), 1153–1161.

Boutte, G. (2012). Urban schools: Challenges and possibilities for early childhood and elementary education. *Urban Education*, *47*(2), 515–550.

Cole, J. (2018). *Kod*. DreamVille/RocNation/InterScope Records.

Emdin, C. (2016). *For white folks who teach in the hood—and the rest of y'all too : Reality pedagogy and urban education*. Boston, MA: Beacon Press.

Emdin, C., & Adjapong, E.S. (Eds.). (2018). *#hipHopEd: The compilation on hip-hop education*. Leiden/Boston, MA: Brill/Sense.

Elias, M.(2013). Educational policy and the responsibility of the school for promoting students' social emotional, character, and moral development and preventing bullying. *Journal of Educational Policy* (Spec. issue), 3–5.

Elias, M. (2009). Social-emotional and character development and academics as a dual focus of educational policy. *Educational Policy*, *23*(6), 831–846.

Elias, M. J., & Leverett, L. (2011). Consultation to Urban Schools for Improvements in Academics and Behavior: No Alibis. No Excuses. No Exceptions. *Journal of Educational and Psychological Consultation*, *21*(1), 28–45.

Graves, S., Herndon-Sobalvarro, A., Nichols, K., Aston, C., Ryan, A., Blefari, A., Prier, D. (2017). Examining the effectiveness of a culturally adapted social-emotional intervention for African American males in an urban setting. *School Psychology Quarterly*, *32*(1), 62–74. https://doi.org/10.1037/spq0000145.

Griner, A., & Stewart, M. (2012). Addressing the achievement gap and disproportionality through the use of culturally responsive teaching practices. *Urban Education*, *48*(4), 585–621.

Goldenberg, B. (2014). White teachers in urban classrooms: Embracing non-white students' cultural capital for better teaching and learning. *Urban Education*, *49*(1), 111–144. https://doi.org/10.1177/0042085912472510.

Goldstein, S., & Brooks, R. B. (2013). Why study resilience?. In *Handbook of resilience in children* (pp. 3–14). Springer, Boston, MA.

Jensen, E. (2010). *Teaching with poverty in mind: What being poor does to kids' brains and what schools can do about it*. Alexandria, VA: Association for Supervision and Curriculum Development.

Love, B. (2015). What is hip hop doing in nice fields such as early childhood and elementary education. *Urban Education*, *50*(1), 106–131.

Obrist, B., Pfeiffer, C., & Henley, R. (2010). Multi-layered social resilience: A new approach in mitigation research. *Progress in Development Studies*, *10*(4), 283–293.

Petchauer, E. (2009). Framing and reviewing hip-hop educational research. *Review of Educational Research*, *79*(2), 946–978.

Tatman, R., Edmonson, S., & Slate, J. (2009). Character education: A critical analysis. Robert OpenStax CNX. http://cnx.org/contents/0a6f5fd9-4900-4ecb-950c-c7391b10c2d5@2

Terrasi, S., & de Galarce, P. C. (2017). Trauma and learning in America's classrooms. Phi Delta Kappan, 98(6), 35–41. https://doi.org/10.1177/0031721717696476

Sojourner, R. (2014). It's unanimous: Effective character education is not quick or superficial, and it begins with caring relationships. *Journal of Character Education*, *10*(1), 69.

Souers, K., & Hall, P. (2016) *Fostering resilient learners: Strategies for creating a trauma-sensitive classroom*. Alexandria, VA: Association for Supervision and Curriculum Development.

Ungar, M. (2011). Community resilience for youth and families: Facilitative physical and social capital in contexts of adversity. *Children and Youth Services Review*, *33*(9), 1742–1748.

Ungar, M. (2013). Resilience, trauma, context, and culture. *Trauma, Violence, & Abuse*, *14*(3), 255–266. https://doi.org/10.1177/1524838013487805

Walker, D. I., Roberts, M. P., & Kristjánsson, K. (2015). Towards a new era of character education in theory and in practice. *Educational review*, *67*(1), 79–96.

Watz, M. (2011). An historical analysis of character education. *Journal of Inquiry & Action in Education*, *4*(2). https://files.eric.ed.gov/fulltext/EJ1134548.pdf

Weissberg, R.P., & Cascarino, J. (2013). Academic learning + social-emotional learning = national priority. *Phi Delta Kappan*, *95*(2), 8–13. https://doi.org/10.1177/003172171309500203

White, B. (2015). Scapegoat: John Dewey and the character education crisis. *Journal of Moral Education*, *44*(2), 127–144. https://doi.org/10.1080/03057240.2015.1028911

CHAPTER NINE

Enter The CIPHER

Building SWAG through Culturally Relevant Pedagogy

NATE NEVADO AND KIM DAVALOS
@n8diggs
@kimdavalos

14 karat gold dookie chains and necklaces with first names. These expensive, these is red bottom bloody shoes. Diamond and cubic zirconia plated grills. Extensions in our hair. Bamboo earrings, at least two pair. A Fendi bag and a bad attitude. Gator boots with the pimped out Gucci shoes. Clean fades and shaking dreads. Jesus pieces. Fresh white tees. Vans that look like sneakers. Airbrushed acrylics. Boomboxes and speakers. Enamel pins with fanny packs. Kangol hats and baseball caps. Tweed tuxedos and Tom Ford. We out here drippin' in finesse.

By the looks of it, Hip Hop is forever an aesthetical power move. Swayed by smooth techniques of the culture, #HipHopEd is thus a stylistic tool for positioning power when it steps into the classroom, the office, and onto the stage. At the foundation, Hip Hop is concentrated into four main elements of performance: DJ, B-Boy/B-Girl, Graffiti, and MC. All four areas require a performance and thus performance relies on attention and attention demands aesthetics. According to Petchauer (2015), aesthetics is a thread that flows throughout larger bodies of Hip Hop educational disciplines. Aesthetics is the idea in which educators and students can find "ways of doing and being," and though has no exact direction, this plays as the strength and beauty to aesthetics as an effective framework to approach within higher education.

As #HipHopEd has been evolving its own identity through research, we have found the need to bring awareness to the developing best practices of college counseling as an integral part of Hip Hop Education. A college counseling framework such as rooted in Hip Hop is not intended to replace, dismiss, nor reject the pillars of Hip Hop pedagogy but rather to inform yet another analogy for a thread that flows throughout our work within higher educational systems and setups. On the podcast *Hip Hop Can Save America* (2017), Dr. Ian Levy stated that the field of counseling has transformed over the last sixty years and can be significantly different from campus and district, even from department to department. We must define and advocate our own work as counselors. There is an urgency to develop Hip Hop college counseling practices as they have not yet outright been defined nor differentiated from academic advising. As more students from marginalized and historically oppressed identities and communities are entering into the college system there is an immediate and accessible need for trained social emotional counselors aside from academic advising skills (King, 2002). Should we not take progressive action to begin the dialogue, even amongst ourselves in the field of higher education, the commodification of college counseling can occur and the integrity of our elemental craft will be sugar-coated and watered down.

In this chapter, we will make the distinction between college counseling and academic advising as it impacts the way we work with students. We will also briefly review how initiatives, particularly in California, can inform institutional policies that then impact counseling practices. We will also look at counseling as a transformative tool rather than an informative process by highlighting the presence of power and privilege and creating collaborative opportunities in counseling spaces. We will then argue to move towards utilizing Critical Hip Hop Pedagogy (CHHP) in college counseling using a specific counseling framework to create these transformative experiences. We will provide an example of our work with a student using this framework as well as providing some recommendations in implementing this work within the field of counseling.

THE CHOICE IS YOURS: ACADEMIC ADVISING VERSUS COLLEGE COUNSELING MODEL

Scholars argue that Hip Hop can be utilized as a tool to enhance sense of self and identity (Love, 2016), promote a strong sense of confidence and agency (Armstrong & Ricard, 2016), and develop resilience and grit to cope with various obstacles and challenges (Washington, 2018). We emphasize this understanding of utilizing culturally relevant pedagogy, specifically rooted in CHHP, because it is important to really define what is meant by college counseling. What is college counseling? What do college counselors do? How is it different than academic advisors? There are ongoing debates within the field of counseling, often regarding whether the counselor's role is to support students emotionally, or engage in academic advising. Scholars describe college counselors as "cultural navigators" as a way to differentiate their role from academic advisors. Cultural navigators know the codes of conduct, customs, dominant values, language, requirements, rules, and traditions (Strayhorn, 2014). Do you get with this or do you get with that? The terms can differ across different states and college districts. In some states, college counseling focus primarily on mental and psychological health issues that impact college students (Dean, 2000). In states like California, college counseling serve multiple purposes for students ranging from informing students with degree and transfer requirements to working with students around anxiety and other stressors that impact their ability to focus and succeed in college (Strayhorn, 2014). As a result, these two terms, academic advising and college counseling, have been viewed as interchangeable and also seen as equivalent (Krumrei & Newton, 2009). However, these two professions, while in the field of counseling, are distinctly different in education, training, and in practice (Kuhn, Gordon, & Webber, 2006).

Upset the Setup: Policies Impact Practices

In 2016, the Chancellor of the California Community Colleges provided a Vision for Success Plan titled, "Strengthening The California Community Colleges to Meet California's Needs." This plan was created by a group of community college experts and stakeholders that found that the community colleges were experiencing serious challenges. Examples of these challenges include: students never completing their degrees, accumulating excess college units, lacking the services to support older and working students' needs, and expensive educational costs (California Community Colleges, 2016). To combat these challenges, the state provides additional funding for all community colleges to engage in a whole-college redesign to examine current institutional practices and policies that impact our students. This came to be known as the work around Guided Pathways where community colleges develop a streamline set of services that allow students to "get in, get out, and graduate on time" (Bailey, Jaggars, & Jenkins, 2015).

In the current educational design, 14% of students complete their associate degrees in 3 years. Of those 14% of students, only half were students of color (Bailey et al., 2015). As a result of these statistics, a major component of the Guided Pathways was to address these disparities is college counseling. Students are now required to see a college counselor multiple times during the semester to ensure that their educational needs are being met. However, many community colleges are not adequately staffed to meet the needs of all students (Bailey et al., 2015). The lack of time or staff necessary to adequately address the needs of all students has forces the college counseling field towards an academic advising model, verses a model of personal counseling. Within the academic advising model, the advising sessions consist of information giving such as degree requirements, transfer information, internship opportunities, and other related information (Shaffer, Zalewski, & Leveille, 2010). This differs from a personal or college counseling model in that the information listed above are components to the counseling session, counselor focus expressly on the social, personal, and emotional experiences and how these impact their ability to navigate through college (Strayhorn, 2014). These counseling sessions typically take a much longer time to develop strong working relationships with students. With new policies being implemented that are tied to institutional funding, the state is challenging community colleges to re-envision and re-examine how we operate (Bailey, 2015). Basically, they're saying, "The choice is yours."

Because many community colleges are not adequately staffed with counselors to meet these demands from the state, counseling practices may result into an academic advising model where the majority of the sessions are information-heavy. This becomes very unsettling when working with students of color. As we've seen in research, there are a number of barriers that impact college persistence for students of color such as significant family obligations (Tovar, 2015), lack of culturally relevant curriculum (Von Robertson, Bravo, & Chaney, 2016), racial microaggressions (Hall, 2017), sense of belonging (Brooms & Davis, 2017; Museus, Yi, & Saelua, 2017; Tovar, 2015; Wood, 2012), exposure to different levels of trauma (Boyraz, Horne, Owens, & Armstrong, 2013), lack of peer and faculty mentoring (Brooms & Davis, 2017; Cerezo, McWhirter, Pena, Valdez, & Bustos, 2013), and the cultural and navigational conflicts between home, community, and school (Wood & Essien-Wood, 2012). Shifting into a new academic advising model, we potentially strip the students from the ability to choose, think critically regarding the information they receive, and make informed decisions that can impact their future, their family's future, and the future of their communities. By adopting a more informational, academic advising model to meet the demands from state educational policies that impacts institutional funding, we may potentially widen the opportunity gap for students of color whose stories and lived experiences are rarely shared or explored.

From (In)Formation to Transformation: Counseling as Hip Hop

Student development theory was first seen as a tool to aid students in developing self while working towards the "betterment of society" (American Council of Education, 1937, p. 39). However, Chickering (2010) argues that the betterment of society is no longer a priority in higher education. In the face of the rising tuition costs and with students believing that a college education is a means to an end (i.e., direct employment upon graduation), discussions about contributing to the betterment of society and self-development becomes less prioritized in their college education. In doing so, this perpetuates the dominant narrative in America that if you work hard enough, then you will be successful. It also concretized this notion of an educational system that is meritocratic, capitalistic, and colorblind;

that higher education is where students "learn to earn" and not "learn for freedom." However, we learn from research that this educational system doesn't work for all students (Ladson-Billings & Tate, 1995). This is why it is important to put a stake in the ground and argue that college counseling rooted in culturally relevant pedagogy is important in the development of our students' capability to navigate through college. An alternative way I can define the difference between academic advising and college counseling is that academic advising is about providing information and college counseling is about transformation. Information can arguably be seen as putting students "*in* formation" rendering them as passive agents, while college counseling promotes a collaborative and meaningful working relationship that provides students with a sense of ownership which ultimately manifests into transformation.

When we reflect on the process of transformation, we envision college counseling as Hip Hop. Every move, every action, every word, and every beat are informed by something whether they be stories, lived experiences, values, thoughts, or ideas. If our pedagogy is the DJ, how we facilitate and engage with students in our counseling practices are called the beats. There is saying in Hip Hop that "a fresh beat today ain't a fresh beat tomorrow." We live in a digitally advanced society where social media can be accessed at the tips of our fingers and serves as a major source of information. We are inundated with information nearly every second of the day and as a result, we are consciously and unconsciously influenced in the way we act, think, create, and live (Slater, 2007). The same idea is applied in our counseling practices when working with students. Our students who enter our counseling spaces arrive with a set of lived experiences, cultural practices, values, and beliefs. Not one counseling approach can apply to every student. Much like Hip Hop, one must always work on their craft. Successful emcees, DJs, b-boys and b-girls, aerosol writers, and Hip Hop educators continuously hone in on their craft as well as being adaptable in various surroundings and situations. To keep people on the dance floor, the DJ must be cognizant of the energy of the crowd by playing music that moves them. Emcees in ciphers and rap battles have rhymes and verses that can get the crowd excited. The same can be said in our own counseling practices. We have to meet the students where they're at because without knowing them prevents us from being able to assist them with their personal and educational needs in a meaningful and intentional way.

Fight the Power

This understanding of creating transformative counseling experiences sheds light on the power dynamics that exists between counselors and the students (Lee, 2018). It is important to acknowledge that as counselors, we hold a sense of power and privilege over students before they even step into our counseling spaces. College counselors play an integral role in the academic success and degree completion of their students. The approaches to which counselors utilize with students have a significant impact on how students navigate and make sense of their college environment and experiences. Unfortunately for students of color, many of them find college counselors lack cultural relevance and the ability to build trusting relationships and rapport (Carnaje, 2016; Lee, 2018). We have been educated and informed by numerous student development theories. However, these theories, especially depending on how practitioners interpret these theories, may begin to construct the realities of students without fully understanding their stories and lived experiences. Bourdieu (1991) writes that this "homogeneous conception of time, space, number, and cause already sets the stage for practitioners to understand identity development with a narrowed understanding of the realities a student is experiencing and additionally empowers practitioners to interpret student development theory how they feel is necessary in order to support a student through their experience." (p. 166). Torres, Jones, and Renn (2009) brings to light the immense power that educators and practitioners hold on college campuses while providing space for students to struggle and make sense with their evolving identities and intellectual growth. This justifies the presence of college counselors on college campuses in facilitating this developmental process and activate this process of critical reflection on the power and privilege they hold in these spaces. However, there is a need to provide additional tools to empower college counselors to critically engage with the active decisions they are making when pushing students to further their identities.

MOVING TOWARDS CRITICAL HIP HOP PEDAGOGY IN COLLEGE COUNSELING

There is a growing body of research that is looking at the impact of culturally engaging campus environments on sense of belonging and its impact on persistence (Barnett, 2011; Doan, 2015; Karp & Bork, 2014). A vast majority of the research using culturally relevant pedagogy focusing on students of color in community colleges exists primarily in the classroom (Hill, 2009; Hall & Martin, 2013; Ladson-Billings, 2013). However, while faculty mentoring and the intentional integration of cultural inclusivity and counter-storytelling occurs in college counseling appointments, there is little to no research around how college counseling experiences help build cultural capital in students of color utilizing culturally relevant pedagogy rooted CHHP (Akom, 2009).

Hip Hop pedagogy has been defined as ways educators can utilize Hip Hop to teach traditional subject matter. Educators have seen the value of integrating Hip Hop into their curriculum which goes beyond just rap music and videos, but also dress, dance, language, and attitude (Morrell & Duncan-Andrade, 2002). Hip Hop is one of the dominant languages of youth culture, mainly from communities of color. Therefore, it is immensely important that those who work with young people learn and speak their language (De Leon, 2004). In addition, Akom (2009) calls to question about the relationship between Hip Hop and critical pedagogy and how Hip Hop can be used as a tool to promote social justice and youth activism in the classroom. In examining this relationship between Hip Hop and critical pedagogy, we argue that from this interconnectedness comes an invaluable set of tools to further inform and redefine college counseling practices.

This is a major cultural shift in college counseling as the success outcomes for students in colleges and universities revolves around degree completion and transfer rates. Tinto's (1975) theory of student integration argue that students must go through a process of separation from their own communities, navigate a period of transition into college life, and integrate into the academic and social systems of their campuses. This is not representative of students of color who are expected to assimilate into the institutional culture that benefits those who are considered in the dominant culture. This reveals itself every day for many students of color in the form of educational inequities such as policies, curriculum that lacks cultural relevance, and dearth of faculty and staff that represent the racial and ethnic makeup of many students in community colleges and higher education more broadly (Ladson-Billings, 1995).

However, utilizing CHHP allows us to examine how identity and the intersectionalities of race, class, and gender have a significant impact on college and career readiness. For example, the focus on educating men of color around the transfer requirements for engineering is very different than the focus on educating them on what it means to be a man of color (African Americans, 11%; Latinos, 17%) in a largely, predominantly, White male (53%) profession (National Science Foundation, National Center for Science and Engineering Statistics, 2015). In other words, our counseling interactions are much deeper than college requirements. It involves a deeper understanding of the impact of intersectionalities on student success outcomes. As college counselors, we have a significant role in providing students with opportunities to struggle through meaningful experiences in a time of developmental crises such as unsure of their educational goal or whether or not their education will lead them to a paying job (Strayhorn, 2014).

Ginwright (2016) also describes this as a process towards collective hope. Within this radical healing model, counseling shifts from trauma-informed practices to healing centered practices. Implemented through the five CARMA principles—culture, agency, relationships, meaning, and aspirations, counselors utilizing this model begin to provide counseling opportunities for students to engage in critical thinking, community building, social justice, and self-agency. Whether it is major and career exploration, processing (micro)aggressions, or practicing self-agency for students, utilizing CHHP can help foster meaningful and intentional opportunities for students to gain a level of ownership, access, and power over their own educational journeys regardless of what type of changes they may experience in the educational systems.

ENTER THE CYPHER

These critically engaged moments that students experience can be defined as community-defined practices that allows for knowledge construction and critical analysis of their experiences (Levy, Emdin, & Adjapong, 2018; Williams, 2009). We can draw connections to cyphers in Hip Hop to highlight students' ability to have access to power and agency over their educational experiences. Have you ever seen a group of people gathered in a community circle to dance or rap? Take for example, a dance cypher. How does one know to enter the cypher? Who goes first and who goes next after them? How long do they dance for? What happens when another person interrupts someone's dance? There is a culture within these cyphers. You have to make eye contact with everyone. You also have to observe body behaviors. There is this unsaid interaction that allows for an almost seamless transition between dancers. There is no set length to a dance but there is the respect that a dancer knows that there are dancers awaiting and that the songs are also limited in length. So, it's important for dancers to put together a tight and thoughtful routine in the short period that they are in the dance cypher. Usually, each routine is punctuated with a strong power move and/or pose signaling their end of their routine. Other dancers also know it's the end. A rap cypher also operates in a similar way. However, it is more calculated as many rhymes are 8–16 bars in length. Knowing this rhyme structure, allows others to know when they can enter the cypher with their rhyme.

In both cases, these cyphers have built in cultural norms that are learned only through observations and interactions. These experiences in cyphers dates back as far as the early 1970s where the youth would participate in this part of the Hip Hop culture. In many ways, youth paved the way in the development of these cultural norms for entering and participating in these cyphers. In other words, their lived experiences helped inform best practices and are widely accepted by participants around the world. Creating this experience for students of color in higher education is important and critical in allowing them to see that they have access and power to define their own educational experiences.

The Center for Innovative Practices in Hip Hop Education and Research, better known as CIPHER, aims to transform the classroom, counseling office, and campus into a cypher for the students served at the two-year community college level. CIPHER is the only known learning community in higher education and located in the Bay Area, California. The program consists of a faculty team dedicated to designing and practicing Hip Hop pedagogy within the diverse curriculum of counseling, English, business, sociology, history, communication, and leadership development. CIPHER stemmed from years of the legacy work from Rock the School Bells, the first institutionalized Hip Hop educational conference on the West Coast.

The SWAG Framework

Once CIPHER was created, our faculty team took a step back and reflected on our pedagogy, as well as our counseling philosophy. *S.W.A.G.* was originally devised as a personal college counseling philosophy that soon gained attention and was adopted into our division's counselor training. This counseling framework was crafted out of the desire to navigate and explain a college counseling approach for working with students within higher education, regardless of what type of educational position or space. SWAG has since evolved into a universal framework that any educator can use and perform. The spirit of the framework's acronym is meant to state how intentional stylistic development of one's own sampling and layering (Petchauer, 2015) of pedagogy, theory, and cultural practices will develop a unique approach of teaching and counseling within the higher educational system. When considering SWAG in this subject matter of Hip Hop education, essentially, one plus one equals three.

SWAG allows counselors and educators to define the way we counsel and develop students' critical awareness on how they identify themselves and how they can carry themselves through educational systems based off of their personal formed narrative. If pedagogy is the DJ, college counseling followed suit as the MC. College counseling is the jack-of-all-trades and wears multiple Kangol hats and baseball caps. College counseling can be your hype woman/man, can pump up the crowd, can freestyle to the breakbeat, can coordinate the event, and can do it all with dexterity and flyness. Similar to Hip Hop's four elements, college counselors pursue these four core developmental elements for themselves and students: (1) Self—Creating an ongoing awareness of the intersections of our identity/ies, (2) Why—Reflecting on an individual's motivation(s) to pursue ideal goal(s) and vision(s), (3) Agency—Establishing self-efficacy to understand and utilize resources to accomplish goal(s), and (4) Grit—Affirming and acknowledging the importance of intrinsic resiliency.

Self. Who are you? How does one understand the intersectionality of their own identity/ies? Rooted in transnational feminism and Akom's (2009) CHHP model, SWAG acknowledges the importance of having counselors and students assess the intersection of their various identities in order to move forward in the process of this counseling framework (Yuval-Davis, 2006). Having an awareness of the ways our multiple identities exist and shift in complex ways throughout our lives and in physical spaces (Museus, Yi, & Saelua, 2017). Processing through inherited, adopted, and chosen identities will help to answer the next guided elements of SWAG. If counselors and students are unaware of their overt and covert influences on their world perspective and experiences, completing the discovery process of SWAG will be a significant challenge to accomplish.

When addressing "self" it is necessary to apply a model of identity formation that can help guide counselors on processing main identities. A suggested model to use when considering identity formation is the ADDRESSING model created by Pamela Hays and colleagues (2007). The ADDRESSING model highlights nine major areas of cultural influence and impact on the ways an individual may label themself and the narratives they exist within. The nine areas of identity are: Age and Generation, Developmental Disability, Disability (Acquired), Religion, Ethnicity and Race, Socioeconimic Status, Sexual Orientation, Indigenous Population, National Origin and Language, Gender. Outside of Hays et al. (20067), other identity development frameworks exists such as the Model of Multiple Dimensions of Identity (Jones & McEwen, 2000).

Why. What is your motivation to progress within education? Why are you here? Once the ongoing exercise of reflection of identity formation is established, there will be a natural progression to SWAG of asking, "what is your why?" Whether asking this question for the establishment of your own counseling theoretical framework or asking this question to a student in order to establish their motivations for pursuing a higher education, it is the "why" that will serve as the heart of conversation. Imagine the "why" as your essentials in your wardrobe. This is the part of SWAG that is not merely seasonal, it does not follow trends, and rarely goes out of style. Furthermore, carving out time to intentionally assist students in developing their "why" will give a sense of intrinsic motivation. The responsibility to maintain the momentum of motivation therein lies with the counselor or student rather than the external factors (Pew, 2007). With the establishment of a "why" there is a creation of locus of control and thus the stage of knowing agency and advocacy can begin. To foster the dialogue of forming a counselor or student's motivation, some questions to consider reflecting on would be: Can you tell me your story of how you've gotten to where you are today? Is your motivation coming from you or from something outside of yourself? Are the things that motivate you resulting from appeasing pain or satisfying pleasure? With all odds against you, would your motivation for pursuing your goal(s) change?

Agency. How can you strengthen your self-love/confidence/efficacy, skills and utilize your resourcefulness to advocate for self and community? The power of SWAG lies in the idea that the individual can create their own unique way of navigating conventional and traditional spaces and ideals. With the spirit of SWAG, a counselor or student must be able to combine who they are and why they are motivated to build their confidence that they have the power to achieve their goals, also known self-efficacy. Our work within #HipHopEd and CHHP is rooted within the core value of social justice and it is our mission to encourage our students to invest themselves in social change using their narratives and education. Human agency is seen as the ability for people to move beyond the reflection and understanding of their world(s) by actively engaging with them as well (Inden, 2000). As Hip Hop Educators, we also see this phenomenon as transforming a student into an advocate and progressing their identity to not only find their voice (with "Self" and "Why"), but now to use their voice. In the realm of higher education, bureaucracy processes can become oppressive and overwhelming to marginalized groups. Both counselors and students must take the next step to develop their awareness and education on how to not only survive but thrive despite institutional and societal barriers in order to reach their bigger why.

Grit. How will you get yourself up and try again, get that dirt off your shoulders when faced with adversity and challenge? How can your resiliency be leveraged as strength and resourcefulness? In what ways can institutions support you in addressing your challenges? Last but never least, the use of grit within SWAG ends our counseling framework and begins with the notion that grit is a concept that is not necessarily created but activated. The intention is that by beginning the process of identity formation, motivation exploration, and the affirmations of self-efficacy will ignite resilience or grit within an individual. The root of using grit as a pillar to the framework is to acknowledge that whether a counselor or a student, the ability to withstand the oppressive barriers and bureaucratic processes in higher education will require an internal sense of perseverance. While grit is a common term used within the Hip Hop Education field, there has been critiques that grit is based from a deficit-model. Therefore, aspirational capital is considered to be a strengths-approach to "grit" and resiliency. Aspirational capital refers to the ability to maintain hopes and dreams for the future, even in the face of real and perceived barriers (Yosso, 2005). Resilience through narratives and experiences, as a form of cultural wealth, nurture a culture of possibilities (Gándara, 1995, p. 55). Despite what language used, the concept of grit in tandem to self-agency is the capstone to a counseling framework that allows both counselors and students to walk out of the office, classroom, or cypher with a sense of a unique take to higher education and into exciting new third spaces.

SWAG as Process for Positionality

"I'm not a businessman. I'm a business, man."
—Jay-Z, Diamonds from Sierra Leone (Remix)

You can teach swag when you can be swag. Hip Hop requires that you make your own stylistic approach to an element and then *show and prove*, or demonstrate, your practice of the craft. We acknowledge that this is easier said than done. Make no mistake that Hip Hop is not a trend, it is not a fad, and it will never be fake news. While quoting Biggie lyrics and playing Kendrick Lamar in class *shows* steps towards empowered safe spaces using Hip Hop pedagogy. The *prove* element is legitimized when educators create their own unique style and henceforth, their own *swag*. Therein lies not only the ability to integrate in Hip Hop Education into our curriculum with fun activities or exercises, but also the opportunity to embody the culture in ourselves and our teaching practices (Adjapong, 2017). Rooted in the fifth element of Hip Hop, knowledge of self, a Hip Hop Ed practitioner develops their own style and their own rendition or remix of the field's foundational core values that will add to the craft. When counselors and educators are constantly developing their own identity and SWAG, the value of "student focus, students first" will be found at the forefront of practice.

To develop identity a counselor or educator training and supervision within programs and the institutions at large must have a paradigm shift towards culturally relevant practice and multicultural competency as a core value (Hays, Dean, & Chang, 2007). Knowledge of self is a necessity for the sustainability and growth of Hip Hop Education, however, many challenges may arise in the process of fostering identity that may stall one's process. Hindrances can show up as the lack of willingness and awareness to privilege, accountability, or historical oppressive systems parts of our identity may exists as the dominant narrative (Vodde, 2000). Even when challenged, developing knowledge of self can be done through appropriate trainings and supervision, accessible cultural information and applying individual intersectional narrative to pedagogical practice (Chan, Cor, & Band, 2018; Petchauer, 2015). As with training in narrative therapy, the belief that individual narrative and lived experience is valid and revered corroborates a sense of understanding and belonging in educational spaces. When counselors and educators are trained under the guise that their own lived experiences and culture(s) matter, this value will impact real time interactions and best practices with students (Carlson & Erickson, 2001). Prioritizing the development of self isn't about ego nor is it meant to call out educators, this is about creating strong a foundation for culturally relevant and reality pedagogy that make #HipHopEd (Adjapong, 2017).

In sum, rather than focusing solely on educational transactional outcomes such as degree completion, SWAG provides us with a counseling framework that provides counselors with a process to be self-reflective of their own power and privilege, work towards authenticity and being critically responsive to students' needs, and supporting youth voice.

SWAG as Tool for Student Identity Development and Success

"Know you'd rather see me die than to see me fly."
—Puff Daddy, Mo Money, Mo Problems

No matter what stage or space within the framework of SWAG, college counselors will ensure that every student eventually walks out of their classroom, their office, their cypher, with a solid sense of learning for their own process of self-actualization and confidence to perform. SWAG recognizes the unique ways that people bring themselves into institutional spaces. As with cultural competency best practices in counseling, taking the time to develop a sense of self and awareness of identity within educational spaces will serve as the jump off for applying the framework of SWAG towards every student's own identity formation (Pederson, 2002). Most importantly, SWAG knows the necessity of visibility and the vitality of the affirmation from the colloquial Hip Hop term of endearment, "I see you." *I see you. I. See. You. SWAG.* When walking down the neighborhood street or into the house party, there is no ignoring swagger nor style. Folks can hate on it, some may throw shade on it, but it cannot be ignored. For students that historically have been outcasted, undermined, left out, and silenced, sometimes the mere experience and development of visibility and acknowledgement is a success within itself. No longer can we allow our students of color and other marginalized students to remain invisible within the institution. A student that has SWAG is a student that is seen and once a student is seen, the cypher will look for their performance. Aesthetics demands attention and attention relies on performance.

To facilitate this process, counselors utilize different forms student development theories to support students through their educational journey. However, as discussed before, many of these student development theories have limitations specifically around how students' intersectionalities interact and conflict with inequitable power structures that result in institutional oppression such as racism, classism, ableism, and sexism. SWAG contributes to the existing research around college counseling by intentionally addressing institutional oppression that students of color experience while trying to navigate through college.

As outlined by Akom (2009), some of the fundamental elements of CHHP that can be utilized in counseling practices through the SWAG framework are: (1) It is participatory and youth driven, (2) It is cooperative and engaging students to research process equitably, (3) It challenges the traditional paradigms, methods, and texts as a way to engage in a discourse on race that is informed by the actual conditions and experiences of people of color, and (4) It seeks a balance among critical thinking, reflection, analysis, and action. In J. Cole's song, "Brackets," he quotes:

Get spent hirin' some teachers that don't look like them
And the curriculum be tricking them, them dollars I spend
Got us learning about the heroes with the whitest of skin
One thing about the men that's controlling the pen.

By providing students of color the power of the metaphorical pen, we begin to create collaborative and transformational spaces that can significantly impact their persistence and sense of belonging in college.

Educational Implications

Given that there is little research within Hip Hop Education regarding college counseling practices, there are several implications of utilizing SWAG as a counseling practice such as creating professional development and training, designing structures for intentional and meaningful faculty and counseling interactions, and creating culturally relevant curriculum for workshops and classes. One guiding model that can help initiate movement for these practices is through Culturally Responsive School Leadership (CRSL). Although this model was initially intended for the K–12 system, its applicability is invaluable when working with students of color in the community colleges. The four major strands of CRSL are critical self-awareness, culturally responsive curricula and teacher preparation, culturally responsive and inclusive environments, and engaging students and parents in community contexts (Khalifa, Gooden, & Davis, 2016).

These strands are so important today as many community colleges are engaged in the guided pathways and meta-majors work in California. This educational reform is intended to create clearer pathways for students to move through seamlessly from college entry to degree completion and/or transfer with intrusive academic and student services support. However, as colleges begin to work on a comprehensive college redesign, educational leaders cannot assume that these structures will benefit all students, especially students of color. CRSL allows us to critically step back and examine how these proposed structural changes will impact our students of color.

Another area needing more research and exploration is how Hip Hop pedagogies explicitly impact student success outcomes since many of these reported outcomes are connected to institutional funding. This comes to question: How do institutions define college success? Who gets to decide what demonstrates college success? What factors are used to measure college success? Do these measurements of success apply to all students? Public school teachers' and teacher educators' arguments for why Hip Hop cultural knowledge should be relocated from the periphery to the core of the classroom would be strengthened by quantitative evidence of the academic outcomes produced by Hip Hop pedagogies (Irby & Hall,

2013). While the strength and power of Hip Hop pedagogies and frameworks such as SWAG manifests from qualitative data, there are research opportunities to further explore quantitative methods on how Hip Hop pedagogies and frameworks impact student success outcomes.

Research have also demonstrated that culturally relevant pedagogy such as Hip Hop pedagogy can be effective in working with students of color; however, there are questions that are raised. Who can employ Hip Hop pedagogies? If I don't identify with Hip Hop, can I utilize these pedagogies to engage my students? There are ongoing debates and battles about who can use Hip Hop. As Dr. Gloria Ladson-Billings shared in a podcast interview, "I don't want you to just use Hip Hop. I want you to be Hip Hop." She then shares a story about a teacher in New Jersey who is doing phenomenal work with students and she tells him that he's Hip Hop. He was taken aback because he says that he doesn't listen to Hip Hop. Ladson-Billings replied that it was his teaching pedagogy that made him Hip Hop. He was able to create lessons out of nothing, one of the fundamental elements of Hip Hop education. In many ways, Hip Hop cultural identity politics encapsulates the paradox. Hall (1996) describes as "the necessity and the 'impossibility' of identities" (p. 16). As noted in Irby and Hall (2013), a major part of the problem is that Hip Hop scholars' obligations to "keep it real," in effect, stifle the potential of Hip Hop Based Education (HHBE) to interrupt the white privilege that dominates teacher education (Lensmire & Snaza, 2010). With that being said, dialogues around what makes a Hip Hop educator should continue. Ladson-Billings argue that if educators are authentic in their approach in utilizing Hip Hop in their practices and genuinely positions their students at the center of their work, they are Hip Hop.

Hip Hop was created by the youth, for the youth at a time where their voices and presence were invisibilized and suppressed. While this article focus primarily in the community colleges, we also see a glaring need in the K–12 system, specifically in the high schools, for more culturally relevant counseling practices. Similar to the birth of Hip Hop, we need to start addressing the needs of students much earlier before they arrive to college. High school counselors face many challenges in their efforts to provide college-related counseling. The counselor-student ratio at the high school limits the ability for counselors to build trusting relationships with students (Perna et al., 2008). In addition, high school counselors take on numerous roles such as gatekeepers, disciplinarians, and mentors.

With this new counseling framework in SWAG, our hopes is to provide opportunities of professional development so counselors can help students facilitate identity development, leadership opportunities, community engagement, and creativity both inside and outside of the classroom. We hope that they can learn and invent new approaches to reach youth and students through Hip Hop arts, music, and the aesthetics, aligning their educational and career goals with topics that are culturally relevant, fresh, and humanizing. In doing so, we begin to center our students' lives while navigating institutional expectations. This type of educational experience leads to revolutionary transformation in their lives (Camangian, 2015). As a result, we hope to develop a community of transformative student learners that develop a deeper and stronger sense of self, gain insight around purpose and power of self, strengthen their self-agency, and view their moments of resilience and grit like timeless 90s Hip Hop classics.

Additionally, we hope this adds to the scholarship highlighting and developing college counseling as an integral part and subject matter to this field of Hip Hop education, research and practice. In doing so, we hope to contribute to the building knowledge of defining what college counseling looks like through style and aesthetics. Just like the spirit of Hip Hop, SWAG is an affirmation that our students are here.

They are like the transitions from the six step to the windmills drop down to a headspin.

They are like emcees huddled together on a cold, blistery Chicago night spitting rhymes that are hotter than the fire that surrounds them.

They are the writers that sprays on walls, carves on classroom desks with textures and colors, not only to be seen but also to be felt.

They are the scientists of wax manipulating sound through scratches and reverbs to create something amazing from something great.

Our students are the community of dancers, the litany of artists, the congregation of emcees, and the local record shops.

It is a confirmation that through meaningful and intentional moments of SWAG between counselors and students, no one's got swagger like us.

REFERENCES

Adjapong, E.S. (2017). *Bridging theory and practice: Using hip-hop pedagogy as a culturally relevant approach in the urban science classroom* (Order No. 10272718). Available from ProQuest Dissertations & Theses A&I; ProQuest Dissertations & Theses Global: The Humanities and Social Sciences Collection. (1896523102). Retrieved from https://search-proquest-com.jpllnet.sfsu.edu/docview/1896523102?accountid=13802

Akom, A.A. (2009). Critical hip hop pedagogy as a form of liberatory praxis. *Equity & Excellence in Education, 42*(1), 52–66.

American Council on Education. The Student Personnel Point of View. Washington, D.C.: American Council on Education, 1937.

Armstrong, S.N., & Ricard, R.J. (2016). Integrating rap music into counseling with adolescents in a disciplinary alternative education program. *Journal of Creativity in Mental Health, 11*(3), 423–435.

Bailey, T. (2015). The need for comprehensive reform: From access to completion. *New Directions for Community Colleges, 176*, 11–21.

Bailey, T., Jaggars, S.S., & Jenkins, D. (2015). *Redesigning America's community colleges: A clearer path to student success.* Cambridge, MA: Harvard University Press.

Barnett, E.A. (2011). Validation experiences and persistence among community college students. *The Review of Higher Education, 34*(2), 193–230.

Brooms, D. & Davis, A. (2017). Staying focused on the goal: Peer bonding and faculty mentors supporting Black males' persistence in college. *Journal of Black Studies, 48*(3), 305–326.

Bourdieu, P. (1991). *Language and symbolic power* (J.B. Thompson, Ed.). Cambridge, MA: Harvard University Press.

Boyraz, G., Horne, S.G., Owens, A.C., & Armstrong, A.P. (2013). Academic achievement and college persistence of African American students with trauma exposure. *Journal of Counseling Psychology, 60*(4), 582–592.

California Community Colleges. (2016). *Visions for success: Strengthening the California community colleges to meet California's needs.* Sacramento, CA: Foundation for California Community Colleges.

Camangian, P. (2015). Teach like lives depend on it. *Urban Education, 50*(4), 424–453.

Carlson, T.D., &Erickson, M.J. (2001). Honoring and privileging personal experience and knowledge: Ideas for a narrative therapy approach to the training and supervision of new therapists. *Contemporary Family Therapy, 23*(2), 199–220.

Carnaje, E. (2016). Advising across race: Providing culturally-sensitive academic advising at predominantly white institutions. *The Vermont Connection, 37*(4), 38–47.

Cerezo, A., McWhirter, B.T., Pena, D., Valdez, M., & Bustos, C. (2013). Giving voice: Utilizing critical race theory to facilitate consciousness of racial identity for Latina/o college students. *Journal for Social Action in Counseling and Psychology, 5*(3), 1–24.

Chan, C.D., Cor, D.N., & Band, M.P. (2018). Privilege and oppression in counselor education: An intersectionality framework. *Journal of Multicultural Counseling and Development, 46*(1), 58–73.

Chickering, A.W. (2010). A retrospect on higher education's commitment to moral and civic education. *Journal of College and Character, 11*(3), 1–6.

Dean, L. (2000). *College counseling: Issues and strategies for a new millennium.* Alexandria, VA: American Counseling Association.

De Leon, A. (2004). Hip hop curriculum: A valuable element for today's afterschool programs. Retrieved May 16, 2007, from http://www.afterschoolresources.org/ kernel/images/aahiphop.pdf

Doan, J. (2015). The impact of campus climate and student involvement on students of color. *The Vermont Connection, 32*(4), 32–39.

Gandara, P. (1995). *Over the ivy walls: The educational mobility of low-income Chicanos.* Albany: State University of New York Press.

Ginwright, S. (2016). *Hope and healing in urban education: How urban activists and teachers are reclaiming matters of the heart.* New York, NY: Routledge/Taylor & Francis.

Hall, H.B. (2017). Deeper than rap: Expanding conceptions of hip-hop culture and pedagogy in the English language arts classroom. *Research in the Teaching of English, 51*(3), 341–351.

Hall, S. (1996). Who needs identity. *Questions of cultural identity, 16*(2), 1–17. Retrieved from: http://caledonianblogs.net/mefi/files/2011/01/Hall.pdf

Hall, T., & Martin, B. (2013). Engagement of African-American college students through the use of hip hop pedagogy. *International Journal of Pedagogies and Learning, 8*(2), 93–105.

Hays, D.G., Dean, J.K., & Chang, C.Y. (2007). Addressing privilege and oppression in counselor training and practice: A qualitative analysis. *Journal of Counseling & Development, 85*(3), 317–324.

Hill, M.L. (2009). Wounded healing: Forming a storytelling community in hip-hop lit. *Teachers College Record, 111*(1), 248–293.

Inden, R.B. (2000). *Imagining india.* Bloomington: Indiana University Press.

Irby, D.J., & Hall, H.B. (2013). Moving beyond teacher-researcher perspectives in hip-hop based education. In M.L. Hill & E. Petchauer (Eds.), *Schooling hip-hop: Expanding hip-hop based education across the curriculum* (pp. 95–117). New York, NY: Teachers College Press.

Jones, S.R., & McEwen, M.K. (2000). A conceptual model of multiple dimensions of identity. *Journal of College Student Development, 41*(4), 405–414.

Karp, M.M., & Bork, R.H. (2014). "They never told me what to expect, so I didn't know what to do.": Defining and clarifying the role of a community college student. *Teachers College Record, 116*(5), 1–40.

Khalifa, M.A., Gooden, M.A., & Davis, J.E. (2016). Culturally responsive school leadership: A synthesis of the literature. *Review of Educational Research, 86*(4), 1272–1311.

King, M.C. (2002). Community college advising. Retrieved from NACADA Clearinghouse of Academic Advising Resources website http://www.nacada.ksu.edu/tabid/3318/articleType/ArticleView/articleId/131/article.aspx

Krumrei, E.J., & Newton, F.B. (2009). The puzzle of college students' success: Fitting the counseling and advising pieces together. Retrieved 23 October, 2018, from the NACADA Clearinghouse of Academic Advising Resources website http://www.nacada.ksu.edu/Resources/Clearinghouse/View-Articles/How-counseling-and-advising-fit-together.aspx

Kuhn, T., Gordon, V.N., & Webber, J. (2006). The advising and counseling continuum: Triggers for referral. *NACADA Journal, 26*(1), 24–31.

Ladson-Billings, G. (2013). "Stakes is high": Educating new century students. *The Journal of Negro Education, 82*(2), 105–110.

Ladson-Billings, G., & Tate, W.F. (1995). Toward a critical race theory of education. *Teachers College Record, 97*(1), 47–68.

Lee, J. (2018). Affirmation, support, and advocacy: Critical race theory and academic advising. *NACADA Journal, 38*(1), 77–87.

Lensmire, T.L., & Snaza, N. (2010). What teacher education can learn from blackface minstrelsy. *Educational Researcher, 39*(5), 413–422.

Levy, I., Emdin, C., & Adjapong, E.S. (2018). Hip-hop cypher in group work. *Social Work in Groups, 41*(1–2), 103–110. doi: 10.1080/01609513.2016.1275265

Love, B. (2016). Complex personhood of hip hop & the sensibilities of the culture that fosters knowledge of self & self-determination. *Equity & Excellence in Education, 49*(4), 414–427.

Morrell, E., & Duncan-Andrade, J. (2002). Promoting academic literacy with urban youth through engaging hip hop culture. *English Journal, 91*(6), 88–92.

Museus, S.D., Yi, V., & Saelua, N. (2017). The impact of culturally engaging campus environments on sense of belonging. *The Review of Higher Education, 40*(2), 187–215.

National Center for Education Statistics [NCES]. (2015). *Graduation rates of first-time postsecondary students who started as full-time degree/certificate-seeking students, by sex, race/ethnicity, time to completion, and level and control of institution where student started: Selected cohort entry years, 1996–2007.* Retrieved from http://nces.ed.gov/programs/digest/d13/tables/dt13_326.10.asp

Pedersen, P.B. (2002). The making of a culturally competent counselor. *Online Readings in Psychology and Culture, 10*(3), 4.

Perna, L., Rowan-Kenyon, H., Thomas, S., Bell, A., Anderson, R., & Li, C. (2008). The role of college counseling in shaping college opportunity: Variations across high schools. *The Review of Higher Education, 31*(2), 131–159.

Petchauer, E. (2015). Starting with style: Toward a second wave of hip-hop education research and practice. *Urban Education, 50*(1), 78–105.

Pew, S. (2007). Andragogy and pedagogy as foundational theory for student motivation in higher education. *InSight: A Collection of Faculty Scholarship, 2*, 14–25.

Shaffer, L.S., Zalewski, J.M., & Leveille, J. (2010). The professionalization of academic advising: Where are we in 2010? *NACADA Journal, 30*(1), 66–77.

Slater, M. (2007). Reinforcing spirals: The mutual influence of media selectivity and media effects and their impact on individual behavior and social identity. *Communication Theory, 17*(3), 281–303.

Strayhorn, T.L. (2014). *Reframing academic advising for student success: From advisor to cultural navigator.* Adapted for print from the NACADA Annual Conference Keynote presented in Minneapolis, Minnesota, on October 9, 2014.

Tinto, V. (1975). Dropouts from higher education: A theoretical synthesis of recent research. *Review of Educational Research, 45*(1), 89–125.

Torres, V., Jones, S.R., & Renn, K.A. (2009). Identity development theories in student affairs: Origins, current status, and new approaches. *Journal of College Student Development, 50*(6), 165–179.

Tovar, E. (2015). The role of faculty, counselors, and support programs on Latino/a community college students' success and intent to persist. *Community College Review, 43*(1), 46–71.

Vodde, R. (2000). De-centering privilege in social work educations: Whose job is it anyway? *Race, Gender & Class, 7*(4), 139–160.

Von Robertson, R., Bravo, A., & Chaney, C. (2016). Racism and the experiences of Latina/o college students at a PWI (predominantly White institution). *Critical Sociology, 42*(4–5), 715–735. DOI: 10.1177/0896920514532664

Washington, A.R. (2018). Integrating hip-hop culture and rap music into social justice counseling with black males. *Journal of Counseling & Development, 96*, 97–105.

Williams, A.D. (2009). The critical cultural cypher: Remaking Paulo Freire's cultural circles using hip hop culture. *International Journal of Critical Pedagogy, 2*(1), 1–29.

Wood, J. (2012). Leaving the 2-year college: Predictors of Black male collegian departures. *Journal of Black Studies, 43*(3), 303–326.

Wood, J.L., & Essien-Wood, I. (2012). Capital identity projection: Understanding the psychosocial effects of capitalism on Black male community college students. *Journal of Economic Psychology, 33*(1), 984–995.

Yosso, T. (2005). Whose culture has capital? A critical race theory discussion of community cultural wealth. *Race, Ethnicity, and Education, 8*(1), 69–91.

Yuval-Davis, N. (2006). Intersectionality and feminist politics. *European Journal of Women's Studies, 13*(3), 193–209.

CHAPTER TEN

From BK to the Dirty South and into the Classroom

QIANA SPELLMAN AND IAN LEVY
@Ms_Q22 and @IanPLevy

As a girl from Brooklyn, I thought the sun rose and set on New York City. There was no place in the world I would rather live. While I still share some of those same sentiments, mainly the beauty and accessibility of rich cultures constantly intertwining, I realize how much living in New Orleans expanded my love for music and Black culture. As a college student at Xavier University of Louisiana, I was surrounded by friends from a handful of cities across the country. Instantly, I became encapsulated in all of their music, as I held onto my own familiar sounds. The multitude of feelings that came over me when I listened to tracks from artists such as Nas, Jay Z, Tupac, Outkast, Scarface, UGK, B.G., Twista, Wu-Tang, Blackstar, the Roots, Rebirth Brass Band, New Orleans' Bounce, to Fela Kuti's Afro-Jazz, took me to another stratosphere! These artists' lyrical wordplay captivated the inner workings of my philosophical mind. While some were often aggressive and even misogynistic, the duality of phenomenal lyricism coupled with edgy and soul-crushing beats literally and figuratively moved my body. Here I was with a fine-tuned introduction to the gritty yet captivating culture of hip hop. Often referred to as the "Dirty South," the sounds of the music simply stated made me hype. As the beats vibrated through my spirit, I felt lyrically pushed to my limits and felt a restoration of self-confidence and an unwavering sense of freedom.

I would eventually come home to Brooklyn with a plethora of hip-hop swag and musical adoration. The exposure to new forms of hip hop, coupled with the revelations of New Orleans' cultural magnitude, granted me insight and an awareness that I never expected to gain going down South. New Orleans was a melting pot that caught me by surprise. Rooted in African, Caribbean, and Native American traditions, New Orleans' celebrations were like no other. Rich traditions and Black subcultures filled the streets on the regular. Spain's architectural influence from the late 1700s enhanced the feel of this old port city, reminiscent of the city's cultural migration. French inspired cuisines interwoven with Louisiana's Afro-centricity metamorphosed into Creole and Cajun cultures, unveiling itself through food and language. This, I was closely familiar with. My Granny was a native of New Orleans (labeled as Creole), and often cooked dishes at home in Brooklyn echoing her city. Her distinct New Orleans twang never left her and occasionally reveals itself in my own dialogue, even 20 years removed.

Here I was, in this cosmopolitan hub and its lineage to slavery and hundreds of years of oppression—with modern day economic class gaps that felt almost uncanny—yet in spite of it all, New Orleans' residents always found a reason to celebrate. Proudly exhibiting a lack of inhibitions, they relished in their music, dance, food, and folk art. The pride of their city constantly displayed through their cultural identity, as their native-born citizens preserved long-lived traditions and generational practices. Ceremonial processions, second-lining, jazz funerals, Mardi Gras Indians, birthday dollars, and gold teeth, all remain cultural epitaphs of the city each having its own specific origins (McKinney, 2006). Amazed at the ability of an entire city to hold on to such deep rooted customs, New Orleans is a city of soul, a place where regardless of the circumstance people are nostalgic and joyous. Ultimately, these cultural imprints would influence my adulthood more than I knew. With a stirred interest in learning about various cultures, food, and of course music, I would later go on to explore these avenues throughout my career as a High School Guidance Counselor back in Brooklyn.

A HIP HOP AND SCHOOL COUNSELING PHILOSOPHY

The coalescence of New York and Southern hip-hop in the mid to late 1990s, would set the foundation for my work in #HipHopEd today. Now as an educator, I am constantly looking for new ways to integrate the richness of classic and current hip-hop with sociopolitical themes, while creating equitable and culturally responsible environments for my students. According to the American School Counselor Association (ASCA) (Stone, 2016), culturally competent school counselors are in a position to "illuminate and then eradicate equity gaps" as they "challenge the status quo and question the rules and regulations that deny equity for all students" (p. 6). Furthermore, the ASCA suggests that "school counselors' ethical codes promote equity over equality so school counselors hold themselves to a higher standard ethically than the legal standard of fair and equal" (p. 6). As cultural and social justice issues often impact the student demographics that many of us serve, it is imperative that counselors are cognizant of both the similarities and differences that students may experience, including our own self-awareness. Hence, "school counselors' awareness of how culturally diverse students may be alike and different from them may be vital to building successful alliances with these students" (Constantine et al., 2000, p. 2).

Subsequently, the use of hip-hop becomes the perfect instrument to inter-weave student voice, cultural diversity, and interpersonal communication. Research has shown that "Hip-Hop culture and rap music reflect the principles of multicultural competence and social justice expressed throughout counseling" (Washington, 2018, p. 100). Washington (2018) also "believe(s) that it behooves counselors to develop a working knowledge of Hip-Hop culture and rap music, at the very least, and to envision how these things are germane to social justice counseling with Black males" (p. 98). Following a culturally responsive framework (hip hop), I am able to interact with students in both a therapeutic and creative manner, which allows me to focus on students' differences and similarities while promoting equity and justice. While I might not have personally experienced the same accounts as many of the hip-hop and rap songs I loved most, the environments, social inequities, and disparities fostered a crucial awareness that would become starkly familiar through my students' narratives.

As a school counselor, I utilize the power of writing through hip-hop and spoken word, as tools for self-expression, reflection, and as a coping mechanism. Specifically, I have drawn from an eclectic mix of counseling and pedagogical frameworks to inform the development of a hip-hop course to support students' emotional development. Borrowing from evidence-based practices such as Cognitive Behavioral Therapy (CBT) which focuses on modifying dysfunctional behaviors and emotions, Solution Focused Brief Therapy (SFBT) which assists in creating straightforward solutions, and Hip Hop Therapy (HHT) a form of music therapy that is innovative and empowering, I deploy counseling interventions to support students in the evocation and exploration of difficult emotions. These interventions are complimented by instructional strategies, such as Reality Pedagogy and Culturally Relevant Education, to support students simultaneously in learning the content and exploring their thoughts and feelings.

It is here that words on a page reveal their spirits' heaviest weights; abandoned feelings flowing through ink. Some need music to catch the beat, others go acapella driven only by the intensity of their minds' own sound. Pain, fear, disappointment, love, anxiety, frustrations, and black girl magic raid the pages like battering rams on New York City projects. Their lived experiences call the shots in this class. Their stories deem them the experts, with journal-filled accounts of their teenage explorations. I am but the reader and listener; the one who reminds them that this very safe place has been created just for them, just for this.

A HIP-HOP LYRICISM AND SPOKEN WORD CLASS

Counseling and Pedagogical Framing

Writing, music, and rhythm possess the healing properties that allow oneself to be free. When considering notions of freedom in urban education, Emdin (2016) argues that youth in urban schools are far from free. Specifically, Emdin (2016) suggests that many of the colonial processes that used to strip the freedom of indigenous youth in order to assimilate or whitewash them are still prevalent today in traditional urban schooling. Our students deserve autonomy. Not only because it is through the stripping of colonial structures that youth can truly learn (Emdin, 2016), but because feelings of autonomy and authenticity are essential in the healing process (Rodgers, 1957). Hence, I have created a class that provides youth the space to tussle with their woes, banish their demons, to stake claim to their internal powers, and to be free. This class, Hip Hop Lyricism & Spoken Word, is their safe haven. Piloted off a program created by Dr. Ian Levy, whose use of the Hip Hop and Spoken Word Therapy (HHSWT) model has focused on using hip hop and spoken word as therapeutic tools (Levy, 2012, 2019; Levy, Cook, & Emdin, 2018), I have been able to offer students a classroom environment where they are able to freely express themselves through writing, dialogue, and reflection. Here, we do not begin class with cultural deficits, rather students encounter a sense of their culture as a surplus; a view that is affirming of their cultural identities, unique skills, and natural talents. Through lyrical annotations of various artists' work and historical frameworks surrounding social justice, students are exposed to the true artistry behind taking one's lived experiences and societal influences and transferring that full energy into poetry or rhyme. This pedagogical strategy allows for students to then explicate their own personal written pieces, as they use music and writing as a form of processing, healing, and sharing their truths.

Following the guideposts of Dr. Christopher Emdin's Reality Pedagogy, students are empowered through the value and concentration placed on their voice. Teaching and learning is, therefore, based on the reality of students' experiences, providing them agency and freedom of expression. In turn, students are able to tackle matters that affect them both directly and indirectly, albeit personal or societal. They are provided consistent opportunities to engage in discourse while garnering relationships with their peers through intimate group writing exercises and a stage to annihilate false perceptions. By drawing from CBT and SFBT, students use the art of writing to address and process internal issues they may be struggling with, as they reevaluate problematic behavioral patterns and begin to develop coping strategies for difficult situations. Students gain an introspective understanding of various unhealthy behaviors, focus on solutions for current and future challenges, and work to build resilience and self-efficacy.

Carving Out Our Space

To further the work, I advocated for additional space in our school, so that our students would have a legitimate place within which to participate in their work, both academic and personal. With buy-in from my Principal and the help of Dr. Levy and a few students, we were able to transform an old, out of use book closet into a recording studio. Within weeks, I was able to convince the Principal to fund more supplies, which allowed me to enhance the studio by adding enough acoustic foam to cover the entire space and purchase additional equipment. Two years later, we would receive a grant through an event students and I attended, sponsored by the Grammy Foundation. This allowed us to build out a new space in our school building, which was even larger closet. Subsequently, we created an enhanced space where students could step away from their worries of the day and "lay down" what was in their hearts and minds. Supported by their peers, one student engineers their tracks, while the others "spit the bars" that speak truly of their souls. Poets are no strangers to the "Booth" or the "Stu," as many of my students call it. It is open to all who want to use it productively and responsibly. Catharsis is my only request.

Curriculum Development

Utilizing music and the arts as a therapeutic measure, allows me to target the issues that plague and hinder students' success, breakdown their self-esteem, weigh heavily on their spirits, and ultimately trigger harmful coping repertuars. Research suggests that when young people experience supportive, stable environments, they are less likely to engage in negative and unhealthy behaviors (Kelder, Hoelscher, & Perry, 2015). Such behaviors can consist of drug use, gang activity, sexual promiscuity, eating disorders, cutting, and suicidal ideations. Without proper outlets and channels for harmful reoccurring emotions, students can be left with feelings of depression, isolation, little self-worth, and indifference (Sanchez, Lambert, & Cooley-Strickland, 2013). Combined with the chore of trying to navigate each day in a white-dominated society, as black and brown youth, students struggle to avoid becoming desensitized to the continuous violence and inequities they observe toward people of color (Huesmann, 2007). Providing students with the physical and mental space to unpack these issues, individually and with their peers, allows them to embrace their vulnerability and find strength in that process (Garcia, Mirra, Morell, Martinez, & Scorza, 2015). Needless to say, their pieces are always emotionally charged, as their range of topics is not only personal but infectious.

I always begin the semesters' first class with "What do you want to learn about hip hop? What take-a-ways do you hope to gain by the end of the course? If you could lead the class, what lesson would you want to teach? What about the hip hop culture inspires you and what are you still curious about?" Their responses always prove to be thoughtful and eager, while often times wanting to improve on their craft. This curricular choice stems from the belief that covering the history of hip hop and spoken word, along with traditions or societal circumstances which may influence hip hop culture, may help students experience a greater connection to the class. Specifically, this tactic borrows from Emdin's (2016) cosmopolitanism which suggest teaching and learning is dependent on students experiencing an emotional connection to class content.

With that, I give each student a notebook, a range of hip hop and poetry stickers, colored markers, and ask them to decorate what will become their journals. I want to set the vibe of originality and persona, as each book will hold narratives seen through their lens. I move on to assign a research project, asking students to choose from a list of artists from the 1990s. Asked to explore their discographies and pay close attention to their lyrical content and flows, students must select the artists and songs that stand out to them the most, explain why, and describe the emotions these songs and their lyrics evoke. They are asked to choose artists that they are unfamiliar with and female rappers must always be included. This process is designed to allow students to gain an appreciation for "old school" hip hop, analyze the content shifts, all while recognizing the power of dope lyricism, its unique artistry, and the transcendence of the hip hop culture.

As we navigate through the class, students are challenged to write about topics I either provide or that they choose as a group. Influenced by personal accounts, current events, and historical data, I ask them to outline their thoughts, including all of the emotions or scenarios they want to address in their piece. Their piece can take the form of a hip hop song, delivering 16–32 bars and a chorus, or a 1½–2 minutes spoken word piece. Students are asked to share out their work, however, are never forced to. Though a prerequisite of the class is that everyone must share out at some point, either individually or in small groups. The purpose of this is for students to gain self-confidence and work through any feelings of anxiety or vulnerability while embracing the fact that their words are meaningful. Ultimately becoming more comfortable as the semester progresses, they are able to relate with one another through their storytelling and candidness. Hip hop serves as a bridge for students to find equity within their own words while simultaneously building relationships with each other. Often times, students decide to take the class more than once or serve as a Teacher's Assistant (TA). In this case, the assignments are differentiated, and the bar is set even higher. Students then work as mentors in the class, assisting and guiding first-time students with their processes.

EVIDENCING STUDENT GROWTH

As I examine the progress made through the Hip Hop Lyricism & Spoken Word class, I pay close attention to the evolution and experiences of my students.

Throughout this process, I have watched students come alive. Here transformative education is not a cliché. As I have asked students to create rhymes or poetic pieces about life, feelings, experiences, and their realities, students are able to assure themselves of their capabilities and internal powers. By creating a space for hip hop to exist authentically, students become empowered, as they engage in a lyrical writing process that frees them. Collectively their peers show a level of support and camaraderie that banishes most teenage reservations of being judged or heckled. Although initially apprehensive, students warm up quickly, as they recognize the safe, emboldened nature of the class. Several moments stand out, which I will detail here. These student narratives will function as case examples that suggest student growth. In particular I will share 4 exemplar student narratives that illuminate 4 student growth themes I witnessed during the class: (1) Improved sense of self, (2) Processing traumatic experiences, (3) Emotional disclosure, and (4) Empowerment.

Improved Sense of Self

Dominique. I am always blown away as I read student journals exploding with candor and the detailed rhymes of their lives. Many volleys between 16 bars and spoken word, realizing they are one in the same. Each student is a poet, even when they do not know it. Dominique, a young Black girl, full of sass, attitude, and fire; swore she was not a writer, said she would never share out, and made no bones that she had no desire to be in my class. Yet she stayed. Baby step by baby step; she would work in spurts inspired by something said in class, but not confident enough to trust her process. So, with each assignment, she opted to give up. Attempting to rip the pages from her journal, I would ask her to simply start a new page. Walking her through her anxieties and reminding her that there was no "right" way to go about this, Dominique began to fill her book. Her writing was gritty, honest, and unfiltered. Still apprehensive to share her work aloud, her group consisting of three other females implored her to participate. They gave her praise and acknowledgment and with that she stood up, delivering a piece that garnered finger snaps and "Ohhhhs." It was at that moment that she recognized her power. With a slight smirk on face and her eyes raising from her journal, Dominique found her voice.

As the second semester rolled around, Dominique selected the class again, allowing her new-found confidence to lead her. This time, she walked in vibrant with a sense of assuredness. Keeping her former journal, she reflected on her process, how far she had come, and began to write again. Throughout this new semester, Dominique lead her groups, assisted others who were experiencing similar anxieties to her own, and had no fears or trepidations. Knowing that she was trusted and reliable, Dominique exhibited poise. Her work continued to be introspective, yet there was a new swag she emitted. Her delivery was rhythmic and captivating, carefully thought out and brave. Dominique's growth did not end there; her behavior in and outside of my class exhibited signs of maturity and self-awareness, and lessons learned. Her ability to manage her emotions and funnel them into productive forms of self-care, while recognizing the root of whatever issues may have arisen, are tell-tale signs of the impact of the class. Dominique has since presented with me at the 2018 #HipHopEd Conference at Teachers College, Columbia University, receiving continued praise and admiration, this time from adults, educators, and professionals. Her sense of self has been renewed. In Dominique's own words, titled *Change,* she writes,

> I use to get mad and never think before I spoke
> That's when I was naïve and didn't care if I broke the yolk
> Bad attitude everywhere
> Cold hearted as a bear
> Thought that's who I personally was
> Never thought of change 'cause who really does?
> When you're stuck in the moment
> Don't know if you mean it
> It's not hard to repeat it
> When your mind makes you used to
> A person your used to
> Or the person who used you
> But time had to come
> Change had to come
> Now I retaliate by thinking before I jump the gun ….

As topics have ranged, so have the level of personal, heart-hitting expressions. Some students released pieces that almost brought me tears, as their emotional experiences poured onto the pages.

Processing Traumatic Experiences

Raul. Latino young man, named Raul, entered the class with an abundance of old school hip hop knowledge, a cheerful demeanor, and an original style. Quiet and quirky, smiley and sweet, when the music played his head always found the beat. Yet to my surprise, the words on his pages were as real and raw as it gets. Never hesitant to share out his work, Raul was certainly not muffled. His political stances and disdain for "45," were often expressed using expletives that created a visual texture of his disgust. Then it would subside as we switched to another topic, where a different emotion was fashioned. His intellectual insight was, not only, impressive but complimentary of his creative wordplay. During his second time taking the class, Raul's writing heightened even more, with intimate pieces such as his *Free Write,* he shares,

The cops come in
I thought someone was dying
But it was my momma crying
I saw a bruise
I saw a bruise
It was black and blue
A fucking black and blue
BOOM POW
Right in her face
I looked at my father
And what a disgrace
I didn't know whether to be mad, sad, or happy
Cuz my momma was safe ....
.... Goose bumps roll down my body as I shiver
It's like a tree had collapsed on me
Cuz no one yelled timber ....

Continued expressions of students' personal lives, their histories, and pains inked the pages. Raul is one case example of how students would use opportunities to write lyrics and platforms to process difficult traumatic experiences they endured.

Emotional Disclosure

Derek. Discreet and reserved, Derek a freshman, carried the class through experiences that left his peers silent and still, followed by soft snaps and affirming "Mmmmms." Inconspicuous in nature, Derek was never quick to share. Yet his flowing pen and acute attention to his journal let me know that behind his soft smile was a life lived. With each read, Derek reflected on his family circumstances, on the unfortunate and regretful incarceration of a close cousin, the death of his father, and the perplexity of a teenage crush. His advanced interpretations and lyrical annotations of artists' work gave a glimpse of an aged soul. In one of his very first pieces, left untitled, Derek writes,

I lost my father at 2 years old
Shit left my mind broken
And my heart cold
They took my father off this earth
And my momma fucking hurt
I ain't have nothing
Just tell me what was worse
For 14 years straight I thought I was cursed
But I had to live with the pain ....

With each stroke of their pens, healing ensues. As childhood memories and subconscious burdens lift, students find strength in their disclosure. While Derek, and other students like him, we're dissimilar from a Raul type student who entered class ready to share, over time the classroom environment appeared to enable their disclosure.

Empowerment

Alycia. Then there were students who crafted empowering pieces that made the whole class scream, "YESSSSS!" A particular subset of young girls in the class emerged as bold and self-assured. Their voices were powerful, and gave life to the room. Alycia is a prime example of this type of student. Alicia is a bright young woman, mature beyond her years, who introduced herself to the class by delivering testimony to who she was. She talked of her goals and made it clear that she was focused on achieving them. In her rhythmic spoken word piece, simply titled "*S*," Alycia proclaims,

> Success, this word means a lot to me
> I'm not a pretty bird with no brains doing thottery
> My way out is not investing in the lottery
> Y'all out here wasting time, man y'all on a path to poverty
> My goals pump through my veins like ice
> Y'all still stagnant over there like a deer in headlights
> Level ups come easy, I don't gotta think twice
> Future looking real nice, lavish living, paradise
> Prosecutor at 32, charging you, it charges me
> I'm stealing the Valedictorian spot, courts call it larceny
> This shit a monopoly, I'm taking all the property
> At this point it's atrocity, I'm getting away with robbery ....
> .... Now I'm hungry to win at my game, Katniss Everdeen
> not playing clean, I'm a grinding machine
> Aimed for that green
> Winning shit is routine, it's the queen on the scene
> I'm ahead of the league
> You'll never see me in your peripherals
> Y'all ain't no visionaries, that's to be taken literal
> Y'all can't see an A and I don't mean to sound pontifical

Alicia's energy was infectious. Not only did her words function as positive reinforcement of her own tenacity towards achieving her goals, but they inspired her classmates to create goals and action plans of her own. Her inherent resilience, showcased to others how they too could overcome obstacles and re-invent themselves.

The beauty and captivation of this the Hip Hop Lyricism & Spoken Word class have brought me to unforeseen heights. With the freedom to implement a progressive approach to learning and therapy, I have been able to create an environment for students to utilize their writing and expression as a source of strength, confirmation, and manifestation. Students have had the opportunity to affirm their significance, release agonizing burdens, and embrace the complexities of their lives. Their fortitude is admirable, a lesson worthy of taking notice and ensuring initiatives such as this continue to exist, yet on a greater scale. As I proceed in creating alternative avenues for students to obtain equity through the use of their voices, it is my hope that the work I am pursuing remains impactful and innovative. Utilizing my own personal heritage, experiences, and awareness, allow for this work to remain meaningful and ultimately infectious. Like my students, my resolve is unwavering, with the inspiration of their words and the necessity of their expression, my journey does not end here.

CONCLUSION AND IMPLICATIONS FOR SCHOOL COUNSELORS

Throughout this work, I have not only grown as a counselor but as a teacher, as well. Utilizing hip hop as a bridge to students' strengths and their personal experiences allows the field of school counseling a window into the lives of young people and a means to develop authentic and creative spaces for student development. Through artist freedom and expressions, students are able to rise to the standards of academic rigor, while engaging in cathartic experiences. Hence, it is imperative that school counselors both advocate for or create programs that offer their students the opportunity to be the experts of their lives and use their own voices to narrate their stories.

REFERENCES

Constantine, M.G., Arorash, T.J., Barakett, M.D., Blackmon, S.A.K.M., Donnelly, P.C., & Edles, P.A. (2001, October). School counselors' universal-diverse orientation and aspects of their multicultural counseling competence. *Professional School Counseling, 5*(1), 13+. Retrieved from https://link.galegroup.com/apps/doc/A80306019/AONE?u=googlescholar&sid=AONE&xid=3af-5cbb4

Emdin, C. (2016). *For White Folks Who Teach in the Hood... and the Rest of Y'all Too: Reality Pedagogy and Urban Education*. Beacon Press.

Garcia, A., Mirra, N., Morrell, E., Martinez, A., & Scorza, D.A. (2015). The council of youth research: Critical literacy and civic agency in the digital age. *Reading & Writing Quarterly, 31*(2), 151–167.

Huesmann, L.R. (2007). The impact of electronic media violence: Scientific theory and research. *Journal of Adolescent Health, 41*(6), S6–S13.

Kelder, S.H., Hoelscher, D., & Perry, C.L. (2015). How individuals, environments, and health behaviors interact. In K. Glanz, B.K. Rimer, & K. Viswanath (Eds.), *Health behavior: Theory, research, and practice* (5th ed., p. 159). San Francisco, CA: John Wiley & Son.

Levy, I. (2012). Hip hop and spoken word therapy with urban youth. *Journal of Poetry Therapy, 25,* 219–224. doi:10.1080/08893675.2012.736182

Levy, I.(2019). Hip hop spoken word therapy in urban schools. *Professional School Counseling, 23*(1), 1–12.

Levy, I., Cook, A.L., & Emdin, C. (2018). Remixing the school counselor's tool kit: Hip-hop spoken word therapy and YPAR. *Professional School Counseling, 22*(1), 1–11. doi:10.1177/2156759X18800285

McKinney, L. (2006). *New Orleans: A cultural history.* New York, NY: Oxford University Press.

Rogers, C. R. (1957). The Necessary and Sufficient Conditions of Therapeutic Personality Change. *Journal of Counseling Psychology, 21*(2), 9.

Sanchez, Y.M., Lambert, S.F., & Cooley-Strickland, M. (2013). Adverse life events, coping and internalizing and externalizing behaviors in urban African American youth. *Journal of Child and Family Studies, 22*(1), 38–47. doi: https://doi.org/10.1007/s10826-012-9590-4

Stone, C. (2016). Cultural competence and ethical action: Can't have one wIthout the other. Retrieved from https://www.schoolcounselor.org/asca/media/asca/ASCAU/Cultural-Competency-Specialist/EthiicalAction.pdf

Washington, A.R. (2018). Integrating hip-hop culture and rap music into social justice counseling with black males. Retrieved from https://onlinelibrary.wiley.com/doi/full/10.1002/jcad.12181

Contributors

Edmund Adjapong, Ph.D., a native of the Bronx, NY, is an assistant professor in the Educational Studies Department at Seton Hall University. Dr. Adjapong, a former middle school science educator, is also a faculty fellow at the Institute of Urban and Minority Education at Teachers College, Columbia University and the editor of *#HipHopEd: The Compilation on Hip-Hop Education Series*. He is the director of the Science Genius Program, a program that engages youth in the sciences through Hip-Hop. Dr. Adjapong is a STEM and Urban Education advocate whose work and research addresses issues of race, class, inequities in education and misperceptions of urban youth. His current focus is on how to incorporate youth culture into educational spaces, specifically on utilizing hip-hop culture and sensibilities as an approach to teaching and learning.

Janine Brown, M.A., has supported youth in the Jersey City Public District for over 10 years using Hip Hop Pedagogy and restorative justice practices. Recognizing a need for more equitable and culturally responsive programming, she founded Brown Brilliance, LLC, which provides SEL workshops for youth and P.D. for those who service them. She is a former Teacher of the Year and hopes to pursue a doctorate to further impact the landscape of urban education.

Dr. **Mariel Buqué** is a Columbia University-trained psychologist, disruptor, and sound bath meditation healer. Her work focuses on the advancement of culturally responsive therapeutic practices that affirm the lived experiences of Black & Indigenous People of Color (BIPOCs). Her clinical work centers on healing wounds of intergenerational trauma, holistic mental wellness, and centering indigenous healing practices. She is also a wellness and antiracism consultant for Fortune 100 companies across the world and teaches the next generation of therapists as an adjunct professor of psychology at Columbia University. She believes in the liberation of both our minds and of oppressive systems as necessary qualities of our collective wellness. You may follow her on social media at @dr.marielbuque and find her work at www.drmarielbuque.com.

Gemma Connell is a British independent choreographer, theatre maker and researcher. She specialises in community dance practice and has undertaken a number of projects to create new dance works with integrated dance companies, survivors of gender violence, stroke survivors and neurodiverse young people.

Kim Davalos is a college counselor at Skyline College in the Bay Area (San Bruno, CA). Kim often works alongside the Center for Innovative Practices in Hip Hop and Educational Research (CIPHER) and is on the advisory team for Rock the School Bells. Kim is also an intrapinay creative delving into poetry, spoken word, and photography where she grounds herself in the value that community art and activism is at the heart of her work as a Hip Hop Educator.

Andrea N. Hunt is Associate Professor of Sociology and Director of the Mitchell-West Center for Social Inclusion at the University of North Alabama. Her teaching, research, and community efforts focus on trauma, mental health, and identity development. She is a violence prevention educator and works with youth who are in contact with juvenile/family court.

Dr. **Ian Levy** is Assistant Professor of School Counseling at Manhattan College, a New York City native, former High School counselor, and the Vice President of Counselor Educators for the New York State School Counselor's association. His research interests include the examination of mental health practices in urban schools, which entails exploring the effective use of the school counselor and other school staff to support the emotional lives of young people. Most notably, Dr. Levy piloted the development, implementation, and evaluation of a Hip-Hop based counseling framework. His work has been featured on various news outlets including the *New York Times*, and CNN, and published in a variety of reputable academic journals. In 2016 he was named the New York State School Counselor of the Year. Ian is the author of *Hip-Hop and Spoken Word Therapy in School Counseling*, published by Routledge. Ian is also an emcee and released his album—*And Then It Glistens*—in 2020.

Dr. **Nate Nevado** is a college counselor at Skyline College. He also coordinates the CIPHER Hip Hop Learning Community, a program designed to provide students with an educational experience rooted in the aesthetics of Hip Hop culture. Under this program, he also founded the award-winning Rock the School Bells Hip Hop Conference which is aimed to educate youth and students about the importance of higher education and career exploration, increase awareness around personal development and healthy lifestyles, and provide tools and knowledge to promote social change within their communities through Hip Hop. His professional and research interests revolve around examining how culturally responsive approaches such as Hip Hop pedagogy informs and impact college counseling practices specifically with traditionally marginalized and historically excluded student populations.

Qiana Spellman, M.S.Ed., is a school counselor and educator at a high school in Brooklyn, New York. She teaches graduate level courses as an adjunct assistant professor in the mental health and school counseling fields. She holds a Bachelor of Science degree in Psychology from Xavier University of New Orleans, a Masters degree in Bilingual School Counseling from Long Island University, Advanced Certifications in School Building and School District Leadership from Hunter College, and is currently completing her Doctorate of Education in Health Education from Teachers College, Columbia University. Qiana's research focuses on the dynamics of school counselors as educators, social justice informed initiatives, the use of hip hop in education, and the effects of racism on public health.

Andrew Torres identifies as a cisgender Afro-Boricua from the Bronx who is a proud father, husband, social justice educator, spoken word artist, activist, scholar, tutor, and workshop facilitator. Recently, Dr. Torres completed his Ph.D. in social justice education at UMass Amherst with his dissertation research focusing on the intersections of raciocultural trauma and embodied arts. His research shows that transparency and vulnerability as expressed through racial storytelling provide pathways of healing trauma within our communities. Dr. Torres is currently writing his first book and starting research to open a school built with, alongside, and for the people of the Bronx.

Napoleon Wells is a clinical psychologist from The Bronx, NY, and received his Ph.D. from Fordham University. He is a trauma and racism specialist/theorist, former Veterans Affairs psychologist, current Assistant Professor at Claflin University and has performed a TEDx Talk titled "The Cure for Racism."

Hip-Hop Education
Innovation, Inspiration, Elevation

Edmund Adjapong and Christopher Emdin, *General Editors*

Hip-Hop Education is a sociopolitical movement that utilizes both online and offline platforms to advance the utility of hip-hop as a theoretical framework and practical approach to teaching and learning. The movement is aimed at disrupting the oppressive structures of schools and schooling for marginalized youth through a reframing of hip-hop in the public sphere, and the advancement of the educative dimensions of the hip-hop culture. Hip-Hop Education's academic roots include, but are not limited to, the fields of education, sociology, anthropology, and cultural studies and it draws its most distinct connections to the field of hip-hop studies; which in many ways, is the stem from which this branch of study has grown and established itself.

The Hip-Hop Education: Innovation, Inspiration, Elevation series will be the first of its kind in educational praxis. It will be composed of books by artists, scholars, teachers, and community participants. The series will publish global authors who are experts in the fields of hip-hop, education, Black studies, Black popular culture, community studies, activism, music, and curriculum. Hip-Hop Education is explicit about its focus on the science and art of teaching and learning. This series argues that hip-hop embodies the awareness, creativity and innovation that are at the core of any true education. Furthermore, its work brings visibility to the powerful yet silenced narratives of achievement and academic ability among the hip-hop generation; reflecting the brilliance, resilience, ingenuity and intellectual ability of those who are embedded in hip-hop culture but also not necessarily academics in the conventional sense.

For additional information about this series or for the submission of manuscripts, please contact: editorial@peterlang.com

To order other books in this series, please contact our Customer Service Department:

peterlang@presswarehouse.com (within the U.S.)
orders@peterlang.com (outside the U.S.)

Or browse online by series:

www.peterlang.com

www.ingramcontent.com/pod-product-compliance
Lightning Source LLC
Chambersburg PA
CBHW071747270326
41928CB00013B/2832